THE GROWTH HYPOTHESIS IN PSYCHOLOGY

COI Psychology

BATH *Maslow and Carl Rogers*

THE GROWTH HYPOTHESIS IN PSYCHOLOGY

The Humanistic Psychology of Abraham Maslow and Carl Rogers

Roy José DeCarvalho

EMText
San Francisco

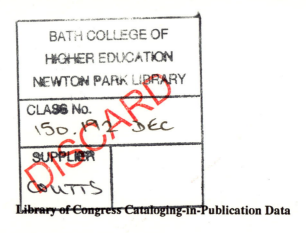
Library of Congress Cataloging-in-Publication Data

DeCarvalho, Roy José.
    The growth hypothesis in psychology : the humanistic psychology of
Abraham Maslow and Carl Rogers / Roy José DeCarvalho.
        p.   cm.
    Includes bibliographical references and index.
    ISBN 0-7734-9908-3
    1. Humanistic psychology--History. 2. Maslow, Abraham H. (Abraham
Harold) 3. Rogers, Carl R. (Carl Ransom), 1902-   .
4. Psychologists--United States--History.   I. Title.
BF204.D42 1991
150.19'8--dc20   91-17536
                                                              CIP

Editorial inquiries and Order Fulfillment:

        The Edwin Mellen Press
        Box 450
        Lewiston, New York
        USA 14092

                    Printed in the United States of America

To

Stanley Krippner

CONTENTS

PREFACE

In an age when many American psychologists understood human nature as primarily a response to stimuli, worshiped the experimental model of the physical and biological sciences, and limited their studies to psychologically maladjusted persons, Abraham Maslow (1908-1970) and Carl Rogers (1902-1987) advocated a humanistic psychology that emphasized the study of psychological health, the uniqueness of personality, and the subjective process of becoming a person. Schooled in the traditional tenets of American psychology, Maslow and Rogers redefined the scope of psychological research through their studies of what constitutes psychological health. Their critique of experimental psychology, behaviorism in particular, and their views on methodology, human nature, and ethics provided a syncretism of the experimental and phenomenological paradigms rare in the history of the human sciences. The contributions to psychological theory by Maslow and Rogers were in a sense an original American expression of existentialism and phenomenology, which found expression as a distinct humanistic current in psychology.

Although naive from a philosophical perspective, behaviorism dominated American psychology for most of the 20th century: a domination that has not been without its adverse effects. The epistemology of behaviorism floundered in a positivistic philosophy inherited from the mechanistic and atomistic ideas of nineteenth-century psychology, and its depiction of human existence did not enhance our understanding of the unique ontology of human beings.[1] The less noted humanistic psychology of Maslow and Rogers was by contrast, from an epistemological and ontological perspective, a most creative development of 20th-century American psychology.

The contributions of Rogers and Maslow to the field of psychology were significant in several ways. Their persistent and at times fierce critique helped dismantle the monopoly of behaviorism over American psychology. Their claim that psychological research relied too heavily on the study of mental illness, which they attempted to remedy through alternative studies of psychological health, growth, and self-actualization, have earned them a place in the history of the human sciences. The contribution of Maslow and Rogers to the construction of a human-centered school of psychology and psychotherapy; a school that concerns itself with the uniqueness and subjectivity of human existence, personal growth, creativity, human values, and self-esteem, stands as a seminal achievement. In education they were paradigm makers. Rogers pioneered the "nondirective," later also known as "person-centered," approach to psychotherapy. Contemporary psychotherapy, in fact, in all its varied forms, remains essentially Rogerian in nature. Group psychotherapy also owes its development and dissemination to Rogers. For these achievements their colleagues honored both Maslow and Rogers by electing them to the presidency of the American Psychological Association (APA). Rogers also twice received the APA's Distinguished Scientific Contribution Award, and on one occasion the Distinguished Professional Contribution Award.

Recent studies of the work of Maslow and Rogers have acknowledged their historical and philosophical place in American psychology more than earlier discourses written from the perspective of the behavioral sciences. Colin Wilson was the first to point out the historical significance of Maslow by placing his work among the most original and influential thinkers in post-Freudian psychology. Howard Kirschenbaum and Edward Hoffman have each written extensive biographies respectively of Rogers and Maslow. A recently published *Carl Rogers Reader*, the dialogues with Rogers and some of the leading minds of the period, the projects at The Humanistic Psychology Archives at the University of California, Santa Barbara, and this manuscript, which sets the life works of Maslow and Rogers in the context of the historical development of humanistic psychology, are significant contributions to the revision of a history of American psychology previously dominated almost exclusively by the behavioral perspective.[2]

ENDNOTES

[1] Daniel N. Robinson, *Toward a Science of Human Nature* (New York: Columbia University Press, 1982). Robinson argued that the rationalism, naturalism, and fundamentalism in behaviorism were inherited from 19th century psychology, which were in fact, already outdated radical philosophical expressions rooted in the 18th century philosophy of the Enlightenment.

[2] Colin Wilson, *New Pathways in Psychology* (London: Gollancz, 1972); Howard Kirschenbaum, *On Becoming Carl Rogers* (New York: Delacorte Press, 1979); Edward Hoffman, *The Right To Be Human: A Biography of Abraham Maslow* (Los Angeles: Tarcher, 1988); Howard Kirschenbaum and Valerie L. Henderson, *The Carl Rogers Reader* (Boston: Houghton Mifflin, 1989); Howard Kirschenbaum and Valerie L. Henderson, *Carl Rogers: Dialogues* (Boston: Houghton Mifflin, 1989); Roy J. DeCarvalho, *The Founders of Humanistic Psychology* (New York: Praeger, 1991); Roy J. DeCarvalho, "A History of the "Third Force" in Psychology," *Journal of Humanistic Psychology* 30 (1990): 22-44.

ACKNOWLEDGEMENTS

Toward the completion of this manuscript I am indebted to Celiza, who has been my most careful reader and sharpest and honest critic. I am also indebted to Stanley Krippner. Without his support I would not be writing the history of humanistic psychology. The writing and preparation of this manuscript for publication was supported by a joint New York State and United University Professions, Dr. Nuala McGann Drescher Affirmative Action Leave Award for the year 1990.

Chapters Two, Four, and Five were adapted with permission from, "Abraham H. Maslow (1908-1970): An Intellectual Biography," *Thought: A Review of Culture and Idea* 66(1991), "The Ethics of the Growth Hypothesis of Abraham Maslow and Carl Rogers," *Journal of Ethical Studies* 6(1991), and "The Humanistic Paradigm in Education," *The Humanistic Psychologist* 19(1991).

Chapter 1

INTRODUCTION

The humanistic psychology of Abraham Maslow and Carl Rogers was an original American phenomenon, despite philosophical similarities with Continental existentialism and phenomenology, primarily because it was a response to the mechanical and atomistic philosophy of American behaviorism. But since Maslow and Rogers' other sources of inspiration (e.g., existentialism, Kurt Goldstein, the neo-Freudians, and Gestalt psychology) were of European origin, this essay examines their psychological systems in the context of the history of psychology. The key note of Maslow and Rogers' humanistic psychology was the growth hypothesis understanding of human nature. The view that a person is a being in the process of becoming not only permeates their critique of behaviorism and psychoanalysis, it informs their views on ethics, education, method, and psychotherapy. Apart from the idiosyncrasies of existentialism, their views on human nature have close parallels to that difficult to define philosophical tradition of European existentialism and phenomenology, which emphasizes the uniqueness of personality and the subjective process of becoming a person.

Maslow and Rogers often contrasted the philosophical and psychological components of behaviorism with their own humanistic views. In this sense, behaviorism influenced, if in a negative fashion, the conceptualization of their psychological thinking. For the behaviorists, at least as Maslow and Rogers characterized them, a person was an inanimate, purely reactive organism, a passive, helpless thing not responsible for its own behavior. In essence, a person was nothing but responses to stimuli and a mere collection of independent habits. In contrast, Maslow and Rogers argued that even if a complete catalog of behaviors was possible, it would fail to describe human nature since a person is more than the sum of each isolated and reduced behavior. In their view, a person was a unit, self, gestalt or whole; a complex patterning agent that sought out and selected stimuli, organized them, and emitted responses that were only indirectly related to the stimuli. A single behavioral act had many different components that could not be studied in isolation from the subjective meaning of the self-defining organism. In their criticism of the behavioristic S-R formula, Maslow and Rogers argued that human motivation was purposive, choice-oriented, intentional, and self-motivated. People have subjective values that provide guidance and direction to behavior; they are not mere collections of conditioned responses. An understanding of such intentional attitudes and motives was an absolute prerequisite for understanding behavior and human nature.

When Maslow and Rogers wrote about their humanistic psychology as a "third force," they were thinking of psychoanalysis as the second dominant force in psychology. They often set their views in contrast to classical Freudian psychoanalysis, arguing that humanistic psychology was a protest or outcry not only against behaviorism, but also against the formalism, determinism, reductionism, dogma and medicalization of psychoanalysis. Perhaps ambivalently, Maslow and Rogers also paid tribute to Freud in their frequent reference to the fact that their approaches complemented rather than replaced Freud's observations by providing a broader phenomenological and existential concept of human nature. A distinction, however, should be made between Freudian or classical psychoanalysis and the neo-Freudians approach, the latter of which Maslow and Rogers especially valued. In this regard, Alfred Adler, Erich Fromm and Karen Horney in particular influenced Maslow, while Otto Rank had a significant effect in the development of Rogers' ideas.

As in their critique of behaviorism, Maslow and Rogers focused their criticism of Freud on his view of human nature. They pointed to Freud's pessimism, fatalism, and frequent attention to the dark side of human nature. For Freud, they argued, nothing but destruction, incest, and murder would follow if one's basic nature were allowed full expression. A person, in Freud's view, was never free from the primitive and ferocious passions originating from childhood fixations. One was nothing but a product of powerful and dangerous biological drives dictated by the individual's past history. The future, at best, was only a redirection, never a transformation of the id's basic structure. No wonder, they pointed out, that the entire Freudian dynamics of personality aimed at holding the id's forces in check, seeking their sublimation and a precarious equilibrium between pain and pleasure. Similar to their critique of behaviorism, Maslow and Rogers countered Freud with a proactive and teleological view of human nature. They trusted the capacity of the individual for shaping, directing, and assuming responsibility for his or her existence. They regarded human personality as essentially positive, social, and realistic. They thought that only when the inner core of human nature was released from internal and external controls and allowed full expression would one become fully functioning and self-actualizing.

Another important theme in the establishment of humanistic psychology is its relationship with European existential and phenomenological psychology. Maslow and Rogers agreed that this idiosyncratic and ill-defined European tradition of thought was a source of inspiration in the formulation of their views. It is, however, historically inaccurate to interpret their humanistic psychology as simply an import of European existentialism. Rather, its development runs parallel with existentialism. When Maslow and Rogers became familiar with existentialism in the late 1950s, they had already formulated the core of their psychological concepts, although in the late 1950s and 1960s the writings of Soren Kierkegaard and Martin Buber had a "loosening up effect" on them.

Maslow and Rogers agreed with those existentialists who claimed that the immediate experience of the individual was required to understand human nature. Like the existentialists, they argued that the understanding of the individual should be approached with the fewest possible preconceptions; the individual should be directly encountered rather than filtered through one's own theories. Like most of the existentialists, Maslow and Rogers argued that the themes of freedom, choice, decision, and responsibility in human existence belonged at the center of psychology. But Maslow and Rogers were also critical of some trends in existentialism, in particular its anti-scientific and anti-biological tendencies. They were as critical of existentialism's focus on despairing nihilism (Nietzsche), nothingness (Sartre), and absurdity (Camus) as they were of behaviorism's S-R philosophy and Freud's psychic determinism. In this sense, they were closer to Kierkegaard's, Buber's, and Tillich's theological brand of existentialism.

Maslow and Rogers' most persistent critique of existentialism addressed Sartre's famous statement that "freedom is existence, and in it existence precedes essence." Sartre argued that there are no essences or reality in human nature. People ("being-for-itself") are a "nothingness," a "non-substantial absolute" which exists merely by virtue of the relation toward "being-in-itself." In this sense, argued Sartre, human existence was defined primarily by its freedom and the ability to determine our "project" in life. Maslow and Rogers agreed with Sartre that "man is his own project." It is commitment and determination, will and responsibility that make oneself. But they also thought that Sartre had gone too far in assuming that we are a "nothingness" and that the process of becoming has no biological basis.

In addition to the revolt against behaviorism and psychoanalysis, and the influence of the neo-Freudians and existentialism, Maslow and Rogers were also inspired by Kurt Goldstein, the personality theorists, and Gestalt psychology. They often referred to Goldstein's work as an integral part of the emerging humanistic paradigm in psychology. Concepts such as self-actualization and the growth hypothesis became the cornerstone of their thinking. These concepts, however, were first developed by Goldstein to denote the reorganizational capability of the organism after injury. Historically, the humanistic psychology of Maslow and Rogers was closer to personality theory than to any other school of psychology. Their early thinking was so close to that of personality psychologists that they were often identified with them. Gestalt psychology was another important influence. Maslow and Rogers incorporated from Gestalt psychologists the idea that a person could be compared to an irreducible unit in which everything is related to everything; the claim that the individual's field of experience determines behavior, that behavior is intentional, and that behavior is the individual's reaction to "reality-as-perceived." In this area, Kurt Koffka and Max Wertheimer were particularly influential in the development of Maslow and Rogers' ideas.

The concept of human nature is the most significant feature of the humanistic psychology of Maslow and Rogers. It underlines most of their statements on the nature and method of psychology and the critique of behaviorism and psychoanalysis. The question of how human nature is defined represents the gravitational pole and unifying element of the system of humanistic psychology they helped to establish. Their views on human nature were not ambiguous or vague but explicitly stated. They were convinced that any school of psychological thought rests *a priori* on a definition of human nature. There was, they argued, no escape from the problem of human nature, since, whether consciously or not, the manner in which this problem is framed determines the questions and direction of empirical research, the gathering and interpretation of evidence and, above all, the construction of theories.

Maslow and Rogers shared the conviction that a person is a "being-in-the-process-of-becoming." A person at his or her best, they said, is proactive, autonomous, choice-oriented, adaptable and mutable, indeed, continuously becoming. Each human being, they argued, is a unique organism with the ability to direct, choose, and change the guiding motives or "project" of life's course. In the process of becoming one must assume the ultimate responsibility for the individualization and actualization of one's own existence. To reach the highest levels through the process of becoming, a person must be fully functioning and the self must be spontaneously integrated and actualizing. Maslow and Rogers believed that the process of becoming was never simply a matter of genetics, biology or the contingencies of external reinforcement, and were convinced that the rejection of becoming was a psychological illness that should be the main concern of psychotherapy.

Few psychologists, if any, in the history of 20th century psychology were as concerned with ethics as were Maslow and Rogers. Their views on this subject stemmed from a trust of the worthiness of human nature. They argued that when people are authentic, experience their inner worlds and function free from internal and external barriers, they value and choose what is good·for them from an organismic point of view. Personal values, they argued, are essential in the organization of personality since they contain the subjective meanings and dispositions that guide the process of becoming a person. An ethical act gives the person a sense of being or ontology, making him or her proactive, autonomous, intentional and unique. For all these reasons, values presuppose a deep intuitive trust in the capacity and necessity of people to value and determine the unfolding of their destinies. Authenticity, freedom, autonomy, commitment, and self-determination (not adjustment) are the keynotes of Maslow and Rogers' humanistic ethics, which are discussed in Chapter Four, "The Ethics of the Growth Hypothesis."

American intellectual movements often extend their agenda to education; in this regard humanistic psychology was not an exception. Chapter Five discusses the humanistic educational paradigm Maslow and Rogers constructed. They believed that the ultimate goal of education was to facilitate the students' self-actualization and the fulfillment of their human potential. Both argued that the success of any educational system depends on its ability to involve students in the process of learning and to perceive meaning in the acquisition of knowledge. Without the student's wonder, curiosity, and personal need to learn, good teachers and well-funded schools will fail. Students are not rat-like response organisms that learn technological knowledge and skills in response to rewarding stimuli. According to Maslow and Rogers, students instead learn only when they seek to actualize their human potential. The teacher should thus make an alliance with the students' natural curiosity and facilitate the process of self-discovery, so that the student may discover the vocation and skills that best suit their intrinsic abilities. Once this alliance has been made, it is also the educator's responsibility to make extrinsic knowledge available and teach specific skills. Teachers themselves should serve as role models, authentic, curious, and explorative; human beings intrigued by the wonders of their disciplines.

Educators, argued Maslow and Rogers, should also teach students the skills, such as creativity, that are vital in any professional or academic field. Creativity is a product of fascination and inventiveness, of inner exploration and self-discovery. It requires the ability to listen and follow inner impulses or voices that speak to what is right and wrong. Only a system based on self-discovery will cultivate the students' ability to utilize their creativity when confronted with the specific problems of their vocations. Creativity cannot be taught by operant conditioning nor manufactured by method. In fact, method is a technique in which non-creative people create. Arts and music education, against critical thinking and method, for example, offers intuitive glimpses into inner values and should be the paradigm whereby students learn to express themselves creatively.

From the epistemological perspective of Chapter Six, "On the Problem of Method in Psychology," it is argued that the humanistic psychology of

Maslow and Rogers stands at the core of one of the most critical issues in the history of psychology. Seen from a non-parochial perspective, modern Western psychology has been dominated by the experimental and experiential paradigms of method and understanding of human nature. In the experimental attitude, psychological methods imitate the model of the natural sciences and study human nature as a natural phenomenon. In the experiential attitude, phenomenological methods study the unique ontological characteristics of human beings. While phenomenological and existential psychologists consider the ideal of positivism in psychology as philosophically immature, their studies of consciousness and subjectivity have been viewed by experimental psychologists as rather poetic pursuits. The proponents of both paradigms accuse one another of naively misunderstanding human nature and the epistemology of psychology. The American psychological community, however, has at least had the privilege of familiarity with the work of Maslow and Rogers, which has helped to clarify the tension between the experimental and experiential paradigms. Their writings on the philosophical tension between the methods that emphasize the objective study of human nature and the more subjectively based methods of study were a rare occurrence in the history of Western psychology.

Maslow and Rogers' views on the problem of method in psychology provide further insight into the philosophical tension between the experimental and experiential paradigms because they introduced an understanding of phenomenology and existentialism into the positivistic milieu that intellectually nurtured them. Although never totally denying the value of experimental studies of behavior, they recognized the restrictions of such studies and method in understanding the subjective or unique ontological characteristics of human existence. Their suggestion to integrate positivistic methods with their understanding of phenomenology and existentialism was not well received in mainstream American psychology. This proposal did not receive any better treatment from the phenomenologists. Their suggestion to submit the phenomenon of subjectivity to objective, quantitative, experimental and behavioral scrutiny was also regarded as anathema in phenomenological and existential circles.

The Growth Hypothesis

Rogers and Maslow believed that there was an essential biological reality in human nature that should be studied scientifically. Both blamed most psychological systems for excessive emphasis on human pathology and for explaining human nature on the basis of knowledge of sick people who sought their help. Rather, selecting persons who in his judgment were "most fully human," Maslow studied psychological health, growth and self-actualization. He thought that he could better understand human nature through the study of the "humanness" of such persons. Rogers, on the other hand, studied people who in the process of psychotherapy become psychologically more mature and healthier and lead fulfilling lives. Both Rogers and Maslow concluded that the values experienced when one has "organismic awareness," e.g., when one is in touch with one's own organism, were an integral part of human nature and thus naturalistic and universal.

The cornerstone of Maslow and Rogers' holistic view of human nature was the growth hypothesis. Both explained that the "instinctoid" inner core of human nature contains potentialities pressing for actualization. In this sense, the human organism has a directional and formative tendency toward the fulfillment of inner potential. In *Motivation and Personality* (1954) Maslow wrote,

> For if we assume that the healthy organism is, paradigmatically, need-gratified and therefore released for self-actualization, then we have thereby also assumed that this organism develops from within by intrinsic growth tendencies, in the Bergsonian sense, rather than from without, in the behavioristic sense of environ-

mental determinism.[1]

Rogers concurred with Maslow. Rogers' notion of "actualizing tendency" stemmed from the same organismic and holistic understanding of human nature. Summarizing his thoughts in 1963, he wrote,

> We are, in short, dealing with an organism which is always motivated, is always "up to something," always seeking. So I would reaffirm, perhaps even more strongly after the passage of a decade, my belief that there is one central source of energy in the human organism; that it is a function of the whole organism rather than some portion of it; and that it is perhaps best conceptualized as a tendency toward fulfillment, toward actualization, toward the maintenance and enhancement of the organism.[2]

In his understanding of the growth hypothesis, Maslow thought that if the basic human needs and capacities which are neutral, pre-moral, positive and good, guide one's life, one grows healthier and happier; sickness is certain if one denies or suppresses them. In this view, there are higher and lower needs hierarchically arranged in levels of potency: the fulfillment of higher needs relies upon the gratification of the lower or more potent ones. The higher aspect of human nature, in other words, rests upon the fulfillment of the lower nature. Basic survival and physiological needs, such as food, shelter, safety and security, belong to the lower aspects of human nature and dominate the organism at the elementary level. When satisfied, however, the needs of belonging, affection, love, respect and self-esteem emerge and organize one's personality differently. Self-actualization, and spiritual and transcendental needs constitute the last category. A healthy person, according to Maslow, develops and actualizes his or her full potentialities and capacities by gratifying the ascending hierarchy of needs. Maslow called them self-actualizers because they sought to fulfill inner potential and become the best people they were able to become. Illness, however, ensues when a persistent and unsatisfied basic need does not allow the person to grow and fulfill higher needs and potential.

In the case of Rogers, his conviction that people have the capacity for self-understanding and personality reorganization, if provided with necessary and sufficient conditions for change, was the foundation of his person-centered psychotherapy. When one is unconditionally accepted and is provided with an appropriate environment in which to grow, one learns the causes of behavior and new ways of perceiving and reacting to these causes. With consciousness and acceptance, the self assimilates the denied attitudes and behavior, thus reorganizing itself and altering the entire personality structure and behavior. In other words, when one explores and accepts the inner self one learns to be in touch with and release an organismic wisdom. If given freedom to become what one truly is, one naturally actualizes the true identity, which Rogers thought essential in enhancing being and existence. Rogers implied that a freely functioning human nature is constructive and trustworthy. People have the capacity for self-understanding, to initiate change in the direction of psychological growth and maturity, providing only that they are genuinely free and are treated with worth and significance. In this sense, the client-centered therapist merely forms an alliance with the organismic forces pressing for growth and self-actualization in the individual.

Some have argued that Maslow's humanistic psychology, and the growth hypothesis in particular, was significantly influenced by the philosophy of Aristotle. This argument could also be extended to Rogers. The fact is that Maslow and Rogers rarely referred to Aristotle in writing or even read his classics. Maslow's rare references to Aristotle, for example, criticized his *Metaphysics*. Abstract philosophical comparisons without historical and chronological discrimination may be philosophically insightful, although from a historical perspective they are misleading. Rather, the growth hypothesis concept, as advanced by both Maslow and Rogers, was inspired by Kurt Goldstein, the Jewish-German psychiatrist and World War II emigre who first coined the term "self-actualization" to denote the capability of an injured organism to reorganize into a new unity that incorporates the damages. Although using the term more broadly, Maslow and Rogers adopted the concept of self-actualization and the holistic view of human nature from Goldstein, not from Aristotle.[3]

Kurt Goldstein

Born in 1878 into a secular German-Jewish family, young Goldstein was enamored with philosophy and literature, but family pressure led him to pursue the study of medicine at the universities of Breslau and Heidelberg. Interested in neuroanatomy and neurophysiology, he explored the relationship between psychosis and postmortem findings. Graduating with a medical degree in 1903, he wrote a dissertation on the neurology of the human spinal cord. In 1914 Goldstein joined the Neurological Institute in Frankfurt where he was appointed director and professor of neurology. Here he studied and treated soldiers wounded in World War I. For long and intensive periods he studied how brain injuries affected mental, emotional, and behavioral well-being. Under Goldstein's directorship, and supported by a renowned staff, the Institute became a world center for the study and treatment of brain injuries. Goldstein's interest in neurology eventually led him to the field of psychotherapy and the founding of the International Society for Psychotherapy. By 1930, Goldstein directed neurological research at the hospital affiliated with the University of Berlin. When the Nazis came to power in 1933, he took refuge in Holland, where he wrote his magnum opus, *The Organism* (1934), which was translated into English from German with the subtitle, *A Holistic Approach to Biology Derived from Pathological Data in Man*. The treatise integrated philosophy with Goldstein's extensive experience in neuropsychiatry. In 1935 Goldstein emigrated to the United States, settling in New York City where he practiced neurology and psychiatry. He met Maslow in 1940 when he joined the faculty of Tufts Medical College. In the mid-1950s Maslow, as chairman of the psychology department at Brandeis, hired the septuagenarian Goldstein as an adjunct faculty member. Goldstein died in 1965 in New York City, a victim of the aphasia disorder he had studied most of his life.[4]

In *The Organism*, Goldstein presented a view of the organism as an integrated whole permanently striving for self-actualization. Severely damaged organisms, for example, such as the brain-injured soldiers, are not merely the same as they once were, only minus the effects of injury. Retaining all its healthy functions, the organism spontaneously reorganizes itself into a new unit that incorporates the damages. The organism does what it can under the new adversarial conditions. The urge towards self-actualization was, in Goldstein's words, an organismic "tendency to achieve the optimal performance of the total organism." In this view, Goldstein argued that no single behavior could be isolated from the total existence of the organism. Even a reflex response affects all parts of the organism via the brain.[5]

In his studies of brain-injured patients, Goldstein pointed out that their inability to abstract (e.g, their capacity to reason, categorize and plan) reduces their existence to concrete and isolated modes of behavior which they are unable to transcend. This condition has a splitting effect on the personality structure and is an impairment to self-actualization. Because of the lack of perspective and inability to transcend their concrete conditions, they perceive the danger to their existence as a very real thing. The anxiety generated from that process often results in catastrophic breakdowns.

Maslow acknowledged his debt to Goldstein in the prefaces of all his major works, often lavishly praising *The Organism* as an extremely important treatise. In his magnum opus, *Motivation and Personality*, Maslow noted that Goldstein "influenced my thinking very profoundly and continues to do so." He also dedicated his other classic, *The Psychology of Being*, to Goldstein.[6] Impressed by Goldstein's broad philosophical discourse based on solid bio-

logical grounds, Maslow credited Goldstein with inspiring the essential features of his thought. Goldstein's organismic views, wrote Maslow, paved the
way for his own synthesis of the holistic psychologies of the Gestalt school
and the dynamic psychologies of Freud and the neo-Freudians. From Goldstein he borrowed the conviction that the organism is trustworthy, self-
protecting and self-governing. Maslow further credited his laws of the organization and structure of the personality syndrome to Goldstein's understanding of the organism as a highly organized and interdependent unit, noting
also that his distinction between coping and expressive behavior followed
Goldstein's distinction between striving and becoming. More broadly,
Maslow implied that the theoretical formulation of his hierarchy of needs in
human motivation was inspired by Goldstein's view that specific needs are
arranged in some sort of structure and relationship and that the gratification
of these needs leads toward positive growth and self-actualization.[7]

Maslow was most profoundly influenced by Goldstein's research on
brain-injured patients. He often compared the brain-injured soldiers' com-
pulsive obsession to dichotomize and rubricize, their inability to abstract and
their tendency to reduce thinking to the concrete, with the behaviorists' stress
on predictability, control, lawfulness and structure. Since the brain-injured
soldiers could not think in terms of general categories, they were unable to
integrate separate phenomena in a coherent whole. When they saw a color,
for example, they saw it in isolation from other colors or any other category.
This phenomenon represents "selective attention" or "obsessional neurosis" at
its best, wrote Maslow, who compared it to B. F. Skinner's stress on predictability, control, lawfulness, and structure. In both cases the subjects maintain
equilibrium by avoiding what is strange and unfamiliar to them. Both the
brain-injured soldiers and the behaviorists neatly arrange and order their
restricted worlds, ensuring that changes will not occur, e.g., they narrow their
worlds in order to avoid problems that they are unable to handle.[8] Rogers
also often referred to Goldstein's work with brain-injured patients as the

primary inspiration in the formulation of his concept of actualizing tendency, although his reference to Goldstein was much broader in scope than Maslow's.[9]

Rogers and Maslow were certainly aware of how much their respective views shared in common, often drawing parallels between their psychological thought and lavishly praising each other. Maslow's first reference to Rogers in 1951 noted that Rogers' concept of growth is "indistinguishable from self-actualization." In *Motivation and Personality* Maslow acknowledged his indebtedness to Rogers' version of the growth hypothesis and his understanding of the essential features of client-centered psychotherapy. When once asked for a bibliography on self-actualization, he referred to Rogers' *On Becoming a Person*. Rogers' essay, "The Concept of the Fully Functioning Person," which he mailed to Maslow in mimeographed form, left a deep impression on Maslow. Maslow thereafter often drew close parallels between the Rogerian concepts advocated in that paper and his own views. Maslow argued that Rogers' remarks on the characteristic "openness to experience" of the "fully functioning person" was a good description of his own understanding of the psychological health of self-actualizers. Maslow also often drew parallels between the non-intruding but helpful, loving concern of the therapist for the patient, which he advocated, and Rogers' non-directive client-centered psychotherapy. He illustrated his notion of the taoistic therapist with the "unconditional positive regard" of the Rogerian therapist. Conversely, Rogers recognized that his understanding of the self-fulfilling person as an individual who, in the process of becoming, is "that self which one truly is," was similar to Maslow's conclusions on the psychological health of self-actualizers. In 1961 when they participated in the Personality Theory and Counseling Practice conference at the University of Florida, Rogers and Maslow publicly acknowledged that they were in complete agreement concerning Maslow's postulation of an "instinctoid" inner core in human nature that is striving for self-actualization. They again publicly acknowledged these philosophical similarities in 1959 in the papers presented at the American Psychological Association (APA) Cincinnati Symposium on Existential Psychology organized by Rollo May. In all of their writings Maslow and Rogers each consistently identified the contribution of the other with the emerging humanistic paradigm in psychology.[10]

On the Institutionalization of Humanistic Psychology

Both Rogers and Maslow were involved in the advancement of humanistic psychology as an organized discipline within the psychological profession. The *Journal of Humanistic Psychology* (*JHP*) and the Association for Humanistic Psychology (AHP) were, in part, products of their leadership. When Rollo May organized the Symposium on Existential Psychology at the APA-Cincinnati meeting of 1959, Random House invited May to publish the papers. This event cemented the identification of Rogers, Maslow, May, and Gordon Allport with an American brand of existential psychology. In the mid-1960s, this group of thinkers began referring to themselves as a "third force," or humanistic psychology, a term first coined by Allport in 1930. In 1963 Rogers helped Maslow and Anthony Sutich to establish the AHP. Rogers declined the offer to serve as its first president. Maslow and Rogers also participated at the founding theoretical conference held in Old Saybrook in 1964, and later at most of the annual conferences of the Association for Humanistic Psychology. They were among the first authors published in the *JHP* and remained on the journal's board of editors until their deaths.[11]

By the late 1940s, Maslow was recognized as a talented experimental psychologist, but as he began exploring "unconventional" subjects he was ostracized by the psychological community. Maslow blamed this situation on the dominant behavioristic orientation in psychology. He pointed out, for instance, that it was increasingly hard for him to publish in the mainstream journals of the APA.[12] As a result Maslow began contacting psychologists discontent with the mainstream orientation, and in 1954 compiled a mailing list of about 125 names to provide a means of exchanging mimeographed copies of their respective writings. Over the years the mailing list grew. In the early 1960s the people on this list became the first subscribers to the *JHP* and members of the AHP. Dissatisfied with the theory and practice of orthodox behavioristic science, Maslow's colleagues slowly emerged as a distinct group within the psychology profession, seeking the construction of a separate theoretical and research orientation.[13]

Anthony Sutich, who was on Maslow's mailing list, assisted Maslow in the founding of the *JHP* and the AHP. In the mid-1950s, Maslow and Sutich corresponded regarding the inefficiency of the mailing list as a means of communication. Sutich wrote Maslow that many on the list had suggested that a journal be established. Maslow replied that "such a journal is very badly needed," and suggested some possible titles as "Being and Becoming," "Psychological Growth" and "Personality Development." In further correspondence Maslow advised Sutich on how he might proceed in organizing a journal and promised to "scout around as actively as I have time for help and money."[14] They soon assembled a board of editors that, in addition to Goldstein, May, and Rogers, included Lewis Mumford, Erich Fromm, Andras Angyal and Clark Moustakas. The publication's name, *Journal of Humanistic Psychology*, was suggested by Stephen Cohen, a senior psychology student at Brandeis who was also Maslow's son-in-law. With Sutich as the editor, the first issue of the *JHP* appeared in the spring of 1961. Its initial subscribers were people on Maslow's mailing list.[15] It then became obvious that the subscribers to the *JHP* needed their own association. With the help of a small grant arranged by Allport, the AHP was founded at a meeting in Philadelphia in the summer of 1963. It was a high-spirited gathering of about seventy-five participants. Maslow opened the meeting by commenting on the narrowness and exclusiveness of psychoanalysis and behaviorism, or what he called "low-ceiling psychology." The second annual meeting of the AHP in Los Angeles in September of 1964 convened twice as many members--about two hundred.[16]

The emerging organization of humanistic psychology reached a peak at the conference held in November 1964 in a small country inn at Old Saybrook, Connecticut. Maslow, Rogers, Allport, May, Bugental, and other well known "discontents," (Barzun, Buhler, Kelly, Moustakas, Murphy and Murray) were present. The presentations dealt with the basic theoretical issues posed by the "new psychology." The papers presented at the conference were published in the *JHP*.[17]

By 1968 Maslow was convinced that humanistic psychology was "already established as a viable third alternative" in American psychology. He admitted that this humanistic trend represented a new *weltanschauung* that would bring "new ways of perceiving and thinking, new images of man and of society, new conceptions of ethics and of values, new directions in which to move."[18]

On the Human Potential Movement

The contributions of Maslow and Rogers were not only theoretical in nature. In fact few thinkers in the history of modern psychology were as actively committed to social issues as were Maslow and Rogers. Both sought to improve not only individual lives but also society at large. Rogers was at the forefront of the "encounter group" phenomena and toward the end of his life was active in bringing conflicting factions from Ireland, South Africa, and Central America together to share their frustrations. He also conducted many workshops in the Soviet Union. Maslow, on the other hand, wrote on the implementation of a society that would foster the self-actualization of its members. In *Eupsychian Management* (1965), Maslow ventured into the new field of organizational psychology. Under the assumption that he could not significantly improve the world through individual psychotherapy, Maslow presented the idea of a "Eupsychia" or good psychological management. He used the term Eupsychia to describe the culture that would be generated by a thousand or so self-actualizing persons living in a sheltered environment free from external interference. Both Maslow and Rogers were also actively committed to racial justice during their respective terms as presidents of the APA. Both headed a group of eighteen who in 1968 drafted and circulated among APA members a letter on "Psychologists for Social Involvement," which represented a call to action on racial issues.[19]

The growth hypothesis of Maslow and Rogers also served as the breeding ground for the human potential movement. At first they were proud of the cultural impact of their ideas. But when extremists of the counter-culture sought nirvana through substance-induced altered states of mind, and self-actualization "now," Maslow and Rogers, grew uneasy and sought to distance themselves from these extremists. Maslow and Rogers were critical of the counter-culture's lack of rationalism and intellectual rigor and its emphasis on spontaneous experientialism to quicken self-actualization, induce peak-experiences, and attain immediate nirvana. Hoffman vividly described Maslow's workshops at Esalen, where he criticized the anti-intellectual spirit of the American counter-culture of the 1960s. Rogers too, wrote about some of these issues in his paper, "Some Questions and Challenges Facing a Humanistic Psychology."[20]

Conclusion

Maslow and Rogers established themselves at the forefront of those psychologists who were discontent with behaviorism and psychoanalysis. In doing so, they laid the groundwork for a humanistic alternative in American psychology. Drawing intellectual inspiration from the growth hypothesis of Goldstein, Maslow and Rogers' contributions to psychology stand at the crossroads of the experimental and experiential paradigms in the human sciences. Although they were well acquainted with the experimental tradition that intellectually nurtured them, they were the American thinkers whose psychological views were most closely identified with the European tradition of phenomenological and existential psychology. In this sense, their humanistic psychology was a most creative expression of post-Freudian psychology.

The attention paid to Abraham Maslow and Carl Rogers in the following pages should not distract us from the contributions of the many other humanistic psychologists who helped to establish the American Association for Humanistic Psychology and Division 32 of the American Psychological Association. Other important pillars of humanistic psychology include the personality theorists and those psychologists and psychiatrists who shared an intellectual affinity with the existential and phenomenological tradition in European philosophy.

In its early years, the members of the Association for Humanistic Psychology included psychologists sympathetic to the classical phenomenological orientation; dialogical-religious, secular, and psychological emphases of existentialism; Gestalt psychology; person-oriented neo-Freudians; the organismic psychology of Kurt Goldstein; the contemporary contributions of American personality psychologists; and, psychology oriented-theologians. Finally, we find traces of the hippie counter-culture of the 1960s, the human potential movement, and the Esalen phenomena, from whom the more academically oriented humanistic psychologists sought to distance themselves. Indeed, at first the only common ground shared by the founding members of the AHP was a willingness to do something about their deep dissatisfaction with the domineering presence of behaviorism and psychoanalysis in mid-century American psychology. When humanistic psychology came to maturity, however, affirmative statements replaced mere protest and a number of humanistic psychologists stood out either because of their leadership roles or because their psychological thought was sought for intellectual inspiration and legitimization. The growth hypothesis of Maslow and Rogers, the personality theories of Gordon Allport, Henry Murray, Gardner Murphy and Clark Moustakas, and the existential and phenomenological-oriented psychologists such as Rollo May and James Bugental were some of those that came to the forefront of humanistic psychology.

ENDNOTES

[1] Maslow, *Motivation and Personality* (New York: Harper, 1954), p. 116.

[2] Rogers, "The Actualizing Tendency in Relation to 'Motives' and to Consciousness," in M. Jones (Ed.), *Nebraska Symposium on Motivation* (Lincoln: University of Nebraska Press, 1963), p. 6.

[3] Stanley D. Ivie, "Was Maslow an Aristotelian?," *The Psychological Record* 36 (1986): 19-26. For Maslow on Aristotle see, for example, the indexed references in *Motivation and Personality*.

[4] Joseph I. Meiers, *Kurt Goldstein Bibliography 1903-1958* (Washington: American Documentation Institute, Doc. 5816); "Papers in Honor of Kurt Goldstein," *Journal of Individual Psychology* 15 (1959): 1-19; Marianne L. Simmel, (Ed.) *The Reach of Mind: Essays in Memory of Kurt Goldstein* (New York: Springer, 1968); Herbert Spiegelberg, *Phenomenology in Psychology and Psychiatry* (Evanston: Northwestern University Press, 1972), pp. 301-18; Kurt Goldstein, "Notes On the Development of My Concepts," *Journal of Individual Psychology* 15 (1959): 5-14; E. W. Boring and G. Lindzey, (Eds.), *History of Psychology in Autobiography* (New York: Appleton-Century-Crofts, 1967), vol. 5, pp. 145-166; Kurt Goldstein, *The Organism* (New York: American Book, 1934).

[5] Kurt Goldstein, "An Organismic Approach to the Problem of Motivation," *Transactions of the New York Academy of Sciences* 2 (1947): 228.

[6] Maslow, *Principles of Abnormal Psychology* (New York: Harper, 1941), p. xiii,99,110,416,597; *Motivation and Personality*, p. ix; *Toward a Psychology of Being* (New York: Nostrand, rev. ed., 1968), p. ii.

[7] Maslow, *Abnormal Psychology*, p. xiii; "The Dynamics of Psychological Security-Insecurity," *Journal of Personality* 10 (1942): 332; "Social Theory of

Motivation," in Maurice J. Shore (Ed.), *Twentieth Century Mental Hygiene* (New York: Social Sciences Publishers, 1951), p. 355; *Motivation and Personality*, pp. ix,27,36,80,89-95,109,116,124,291; "Deficiency Motivation and Growth Motivation," in M. R. Jones (Ed.), *Nebraska Symposium in Motivation* (Lincoln: University of Nebraska Press, 1955), p. 5; "Mental Health and Religion," in *Academy of Religion, Science and Mental Health* (New York: New York University Press, 1959), p. 19; *Toward a Psychology of Being*, p. v; *Religion, Values and Peak-Experiences* (Columbus: Ohio State University Press, 1964), p. 64; "Foreword," in Andras Angyal, *Neurosis and Treatment: A Holistic Theory* (New York: Wiley, 1965), p. v; *Farther Reaches of Human Nature* (New York: Viking, 1971), pp. 32,119. A. Maslow and D. MacKinnon, "Personality," in Harry Helson (Ed.), *Theoretical Foundations of Psychology* (New York: Van Nostrand, 1951), pp. 645.

[8] Maslow, *Abnormal Psychology*, p. 18; "Psychological Security-Insecurity," p. 332; *Motivation and Personality*, 95,161,166,192,206,262,286, 296; *Religion, Values and Peak-Experiences*, pp. 16,79; *The Psychology of Science* (New York: Harper & Row, 1966), pp. 23-26,69; *Reaches of Human Nature*, p. 252.

[9] Rogers, *Client-Centered Therapy* (Boston: Houghton Mifflin, 1951), pp. 481,489; "Client-Centered Therapy," in S. Arieti (Ed.), *American Handbook of Psychiatry* (New York: Basic Books, 1959), vol. 3, pp. 183-200; "The Actualizing Tendency," p. 3; "Foundations of the Person-Centered Approach," *Education* 100 (1979): 98-100.

[10] Hoffman, *The Right To Be*, p. 261. Maslow & MacKinnon, "Personality," p. 646. Maslow, *Motivation and Personality*, 116,124,142,240,342,390; "Power Relationship and Patterns of Personal Development," in A. Kornhauser (Ed.) *Problems of Power in American Democracy* (Detroit: Wayne State University, 1957), pp. 99,124; "Some Frontier Problems in Mental Health," in A. Combs (Ed.), *Personality Theory and Counseling Practice* (Miami: University of Florida Press, 1961), pp. 5,6,10; *Psychology of Being*, pp. 25,38,48,105,137,138,197; "A Dialogue with Abraham H. Maslow," *Journal of Humanistic Psychology* 19 (1979): 26-27; *Religion, Values and Peak-Experiences*, pp. 16,100; *The Psychology of Science*, p. 104; "Comments on Dr. Frankl's Paper," *Journal of Humanistic Psychology* 6 (1966): 108; "Dialogue on Communication," in A. Hitchcock (Ed.), *Guidance and the Utilization of New Educational Media* (Washington, DC: American Personnel and Guidance Association, 1967), p. 21; "Conversation with Abraham H. Maslow," *Psychology Today* 2 (1968): 55; *Reaches of Human Nature*, pp. 32,42,73,113,116,166,139, 163,187,189,289,338; "Interview," In Willard B. Frick, *Humanistic Psychology:*

Interviews with Maslow, Murphy and Rogers (Columbus: Merrill, 1971), p. 27. *Carl Rogers, On Becoming a Person* (Boston: Houghton Mifflin, 1961), pp. ix, 174; *Client-Centered*, p. 482; "A Theory of Therapy, Personality, and Interpersonal Relationship, as Developed in the Client-Centered Framework," in S. Koch (Ed.), *Psychology: A Study of a Science* (New York: McGraw-Hill, 1959), pp. 194,196; "Carl Rogers Speaks Out on Group and the Lack of a Human Science," *Psychology Today* 1 (1967): 66; "Looking Back & Ahead: A Conversation With Carl Rogers," in J. T. Hart and T. M. Tomlinson (Eds.), *New Directions in Client-Centered Therapy* (Boston: Houghton Mifflin, 1970), p. 504; "Person-Centered Approach," p. 100.

[11] Rollo May, *Existential Psychology* (New York: Random House, 1960); "Intentionality, the Heart of Human Will,"*Journal of Humanistic Psychology* 5 (1965): 55-70. R. J. DeCarvalho, "Who Coined the Term 'Humanistic Psychology'?," *The Humanistic Psychologist* 18 (1990): 350-351.

[12] Anthony Sutich, *The Founding of Humanistic Psychology and Transpersonal Psychology: A Personal Account* (unpublished doctoral dissertation, Saybrook Institute, 1976), p. 30. R. J. DeCarvalho, "A History of the 'Third Force' in Psychology," *Journal of Humanistic Psychology* 30 (1990): 22-44.

[13] Maslow, *Toward a Psychology of Being*, p. 237.

[14] Sutich, *The Founding*, pp. 7-64; "The Emergence of the Transpersonal Orientation," *Journal of Transpersonal Psychology* 8 (1976): 5-19. M. Vich, "Anthony Sutich: An Appreciation," *Journal of Transpersonal Psychology* 8 (1976): 2-4.

[15] Tom Greening, "The Origins of the Journal of Humanistic Psychology and the Association for Humanistic Psychology," *Journal of Humanistic Psychology* 25 (1985): 7-11; "Commentary," *Journal of Humanistic Psychology* 28 (1988): 68-72.

[16] Sutich, *The Founding*, pp. 89-126. *AHP Newsletter*, 1963 December, 1965 November.

[17] *Journal of Humanistic Psychology* 5 (1965); Sutich, *The Founding*, pp. 127-134.

[18] Maslow, *Psychology of Being*, p. iii; *Motivation and Personality* (New York: Harper & Row, revised edition 1970), p. ix.

[19] Hoffman, *The Right To Be*, p. 309. Maslow, *Eupsychian Management* (Homewood: Irwin-Dorsey, 1965).

[20] Hoffman, *The Right To Be*, pp. 285,288,292-293,328-329. See also Maslow, "Some Frontier Problems," p. 2; "Humanistic Education vs. Professional Education," *Journal of Humanistic Psychology* 19 (1979): 17-25; *Motivation and Personality*, p. xxii; "Interview," p. 36. Rogers, "Some Questions and Challenges Facing a Humanistic Psychology," *Journal of Humanistic Psychology* 5 (1965): 1-5.

Chapter 2

ABRAHAM H. MASLOW
AN INTELLECTUAL BIOGRAPHY[*]

It is interesting that even his parents was neither intimate nor loving and he discovered anti-Semitism he still loved to believed innate goodness human being

Abraham H. Maslow was born on April 1, 1908, in New York City, the first of seven children. Maslow's relationship with his parents, Russian-Jewish immigrants from Kiev, was neither intimate nor loving. He attended New York City schools. At the age of nine he moved to a non-Jewish neighborhood and, since he looked quite Jewish, discovered anti-Semitism there. He described his first twenty years as extremely neurotic, shy, nervous, depressed, lonely, and self-reflecting. He isolated himself at school and, since he could not stand being at home, practically lived in the library. At school he was an achiever, and he enrolled in law school upon the advice of his father. Because of lack of interest, however, he did not finish the freshman year. At the end of 1928, then twenty years old, he married Bertha Goodman, a cousin, whom he had courted for a long time. Both enrolled at the University of Wisconsin-Madison, where he received a BA (1930), MA (1931), and PhD (1934) in psychology.[1]

In Madison, Maslow was still shy and timid, but well liked by his teachers. Fascinated by Watson's theory of behaviorism, which was then in vogue,

---

[*] Adapted with permission from "Abraham H. Maslow (1908-1970): An Intellectual Biography," *Thought: A Review of Culture and Idea* 66 (1991).

he concentrated on classical laboratory research with dogs and apes. His earliest papers focused on the emotion of disgust in dogs and the learning process among primates. In his doctoral dissertation he explored the role of dominance in the social and sexual behavior of primates, arguing that dominance among primates is usually established by visual contact rather than by fighting.

From the time he received his doctorate until 1937, Maslow worked as a research assistant in social psychology for Edward L. Thorndike at Teachers College, Columbia University. His first teaching position was with Brooklyn College between 1937 and 1951. During this period New York City was an intellectual center for such exiled German psychologists as Max Wertheimer, Erich Fromm, Karen Horney, Kurt Goldstein, and Ruth Benedict. Maslow's association with these thinkers deeply influenced the development of his ideas.

In 1951 Maslow was invited to head the recently established department of psychology at Brandeis University, a position he held for ten years. In 1969 he left Brandeis to take a fellowship at the Laughlin Foundation in Menlo Park, California.

Soon after leaving Madison, Maslow became convinced that most of modern psychological research and theory relied too much on subjects who had turned to psychologists for pathological reasons. The image of human nature delineated by studies of these patients was inevitably pessimistic and distorted. Maslow attempted to remedy the situation by studying individuals considered the finest examples of healthy people. He called them "self-actualizing" persons, since they showed a high degree of need for meaningful work, responsibility, creativity, fairness, and justice.

In his epoch-making 1943 article, "A Theory of Human Motivation," and more explicitly in *Motivation and Personality* (1954), Maslow argued that there are higher and lower needs in human motivation. Both are "instinctoid" and arranged in a hierarchy. These needs are, in order: physiological well-being, safety, love, esteem, and self-actualization. Each group of needs relies on prior satisfaction of previous needs. Thus, in Maslow's reasoning, human nature is the continuous fulfillment of inner needs, beginning with those of a basic physiological character and progressing to meta-needs. Self-actualizers, he argued, were persons who had satisfied the lower needs and sought to fulfill higher reaches of human nature by becoming all they were capable of becoming. *as opposed to this notion with they as for 'better people'.*

In *Religion, Values and Peak-Experiences* (1964), Maslow argued that self-actualizing persons embodied the guiding or ultimate values by which humanity should live. These values were meant to be the basis of a science of ethics. In the same work, Maslow concluded that self-actualizing persons have had simple and natural experiences of ecstasy or bliss, moments of great awe or intense experiences--"peak-experiences," as he named them.

In *Eupsychian Management* (1965), Maslow attempted to introduce his thought into the new field of organizational psychology. In that work, under the assumption that he could not improve the world through individual psychotherapy, he presented the idea of a "Eupsychia" or good psychological management. He used the term Eupsychia originally to describe the culture that would be generated by a thousand or so self-actualizing persons living in a sheltered environment free from external interference. In this work he maintained that workers could achieve the highest possible productivity if their "humanness" and potential for self-actualization were given the opportunity to grow so that their higher or meta-needs could be fulfilled. Toward the end of his life, mainly in the posthumously published *Farther Reaches of Human Nature* (1971), Maslow went a step further and argued that there are needs beyond self-actualization--that is, transcendental or transpersonal needs centered on the cosmos, religion, and the mystical realms of being.

During the 1960s Maslow, with the assistance of Anthony Sutich, was instrumental in advancing the organization of the field of humanistic psychology through the establishment of the Association for Humanistic Psychology and its publication, the *Journal of Humanistic Psychology*. He also supported, in the late 1960s, the emerging field of transpersonal psychology.[2] Maslow died of a heart attack on June 8, 1970, at the age of 62.

Views on Behavioristic Psychology

The humanistic psychology advocated by the Association for Humanistic Psychology and leading spokespersons such as Gordon Allport, Carl Rogers, Rollo May, and James Bugental was an outcry against what they perceived as behaviorism's mechanistic concept of human nature and its academic sterility. Thus, humanistic psychologists often contrasted behavioristic and humanistic views of human nature, psychotherapy, method, and ethics. Maslow was not an exception.[3]

Maslow was nurtured in the best behavioristic tradition of the early and mid-1930s, working with Harry Harlow in his primate lab in Madison, Wisconsin. Here Maslow acquired a first-hand familiarity with behaviorism that was often evident in his later critique of the behaviorist school. Maslow's critique, which took shape during the 1940s, was framed by his theory of motivation: the concept of behavior, the psychological implications of behavioral prediction and control, the definition of scientific method in the psychological sciences, and concepts of human nature implicit in behaviorism.

Maslow had a romance with and a tragic divorce from behaviorism. As a philosophy student at Cornell, Maslow was initially drawn to behaviorism because of a dislike of the speculative character of philosophical discourse. Rather, he was attracted to the empirical and physiological school of 19th century psychology advocated in the United States by Tichener. However, in his early twenties Maslow's study of Watson led him to realize the potential contained in the behaviorist approach. The discovery of Watson's behavioristic program, Maslow recalled many years later, produced such "an explosion of excitement" that he went "dancing down Fifth Avenue with exuberance."

All you needed, he thought, was to work hard and everything could be changed and reconditioned. The techniques of conditioning seemed to promise a solution to all psychological and social problems, and the simple positivism and objectivism contained in the philosophy of behaviorism appeared to protect him from repeating the philosophical mistakes of the past. With such ideas, Maslow joined the department of psychology at the University of Wisconsin-Madison, where his entire training and education were shaped by the methods and concepts of behaviorism.[4]

Maslow's MA thesis (1931), an experimental study of the effect of varying simple external conditions on learning, initiated his entry into the science of prediction and control of behavior. His doctoral dissertation, written under the supervision of Harry Harlow, analyzed the role of dominance among primates from a behavioristic conceptual framework. A year after graduation, however, Maslow departed Wisconsin and left behind the behavioristic approach of his teachers. In New York City, while teaching first at Teacher's College of Columbia University and later at Brooklyn College, Maslow read Freud, the Gestalt psychologists, and the embryologist Ludwig von Bertalanffy; he also became disillusioned with English philosophy, particularly as represented by Bertrand Russell. In New York he met Alfred Adler, Max Wertheimer, Kurt Goldstein, and Ruth Benedict, and under their influence the focus of his experimental studies shifted from Harlow's primates to people; specifically female college students in New York City. Along with his research on dominance, Maslow developed the theory of motivation that made him famous.[5]

Maslow's critique of behaviorism can be divided into three phases. The first phase began with his arrival in New York City and lasted until the early 1940s, when he began publishing his need-hierarchy theory of motivation. The second phase extended through the 1940s when he wrote key essays on human motivation compiled in *Motivation and Personality* (1954). The last phase extended from the early 1950s until his death in 1970.

During the first phase Maslow regarded human behavior not merely as the result of a linear connection between a single and isolated stimulus and a single response, but also as determined by all the feelings, attitudes, and wishes that go into making a complete personality. Maslow believed these personality determinants resulted in great part from the introspection or interiorization of social convictions and ethical norms of the group. During the second phase, Maslow made these ideas an integral part of his theory of motivation. He repeatedly argued that the study of isolated single behaviors, and the idea that such behaviors are self-contained, is a simplistic and misleading approach to understanding human motivation. Maslow continued writing in the 1950s on method and theory in psychology, but his criticism addressed only positivistic psychology in general.

Maslow's critique of the behavioristic concept of control and prediction was argued in terms of the need-hierarchy theory of motivation. This theory distinguished between expressive and coping behavior; Maslow accused behaviorists of concentrating almost exclusively on the study of coping behavior, which he argued was the least significant part of personality. Expressive behavior--artistic creation, play, wonder, and love--is part of a person and a reflection of personality even if it is non-functional and persists without reward. It is an epiphenomenon of inner character-structure, the study of which should be the goal of psychology. On the other hand, coping behavior is functional, instrumental, adaptive. It is the product of an interaction of the character-structure with the world. Since coping behavior is learned or acquired in order to deal with specific environmental situations, it dies out if not rewarded or continuously bombarded with stimuli. Maslow concluded that one should be cautious in extrapolating from coping behaviors to general conclusions about human nature. The behaviorist, according to Maslow, sees only the animal-like aspects of human nature, precisely because he focuses exclusively on coping behavior. Gordon Allport made a similar analysis of expressive and coping behavior in 1961.[6]

In *The Psychology of Science* (1966) Maslow compared external scientific control of the behavioristic type with the internal self-knowledge posited by humanistic science in their ability to predict behavior. He argued that people resent and rebel against external scientific control, but they accept the increase of self-knowledge that allows them to control their own behavior. Thus self-knowledge of the humanistic type has much more predictive power. Carl Rogers had written an almost identical argument in "The Role of Self-Understanding in the Prediction of Behavior."[7]

Maslow argued, much as did Allport, that even if the behaviorists could add up a collection of single behaviors, their picture of human nature would still be incomplete; the human organism is more than just the sum of each isolated and reduced part. The parts affect the whole and vice versa in a continual process of mutual transformation. He argued that the person was a unit, self, gestalt, whole, or process. A behavioral act has many components that cannot be studied in isolation from the self-containing organism. For Maslow the self is a complex, internal patterning agent that organizes the stimulus and emits a response that relates to the stimulus through the organism. Human motivation is purposive, or choice-oriented, proactive rather than reactive, self-motivated rather than restricted to "anticipatory goal reaction." Every one of us, he argued, has a peculiar set of subjective values that provides guidance and direction to life. An understanding of such inner attitudes and motives is an absolute prerequisite to the understanding of human behavior and human nature.[8]

Views on Psychoanalysis

Humanistic psychologists have described their school of thought as a "third force" in psychology, with behaviorism as the dominant, first force and psychoanalysis as the second force. Like most of his colleagues, Maslow posited his views in contrast to classical Freudian psychoanalysis, arguing that humanistic psychology was a protest or outcry, not only against behaviorism but also against the formalism, determinism, and dogma of psychoanalysis. Perhaps ambivalently, Maslow also paid tribute to Freud. Quite often, he even referred to humanistic psychology as complementing rather than replacing Freud's observations.[9] Maslow distinguished between facts and theory in Freudian thought; he praised the facts or clinical experience but despised Freud's metaphysics. In the late 1960s, he argued that Freud the fact-finder, not Freud the metaphysician, is still required reading for every humanistic psychologist.[10]

Maslow was psychoanalyzed at least three times, in the late 1940s and early 1950s by Emil Oberholzer and Felix Deutsch respectively, and in the 1960s by Harry Rand. He described his analysis as "the best of all learning experiences" and he said it taught him about psychoanalysis "from the inside, by experiencing it."[11]

A distinction must be made within the psychoanalytical movement between Freud, or classical psychoanalysis, and the neo-Freudians. Maslow and most humanistic psychologists were indebted as well to the neo-Freudians. Maslow often acknowledged the influence on his work of Alfred Adler, Erich Fromm, Karen Horney, David Levy, Abram Kardiner, Sandor Rado, and Franz Alexander. Most of Maslow's contact with the neo-Freudians took place during his post-doctoral years in New York in the 1940s when the city was flooded with learned emigres from Europe.[12]

During this period Maslow met Heinz L. Ansbacher, who introduced him to the informal seminars Adler sponsored at the hotel where he lived. After Adler read Maslow's dissertation on the social behavior of primates, he encouraged Maslow to present a summary of his conclusions in the *Journal of Individual Psychology*. The results invited comparison between the behavior of humans and primates, and encouraged by Adler's support, Maslow became increasingly oriented toward the study of humans rather than primates as experimental subjects in his studies of dominance. Heinz Ansbacher believes that as Maslow's humanistic psychology matured it came to resemble Adler's "Individual Psychology" ever more closely.[13]

The influence of Fromm and Horney was also important in Maslow's intellectual development. Fromm and Horney were, along with Adler, Goldstein and Rogers, among the authors most frequently quoted by Maslow in his works. In the late 1930s and early 1940s, Maslow often discussed his ideas on motivation with Fromm and Horney, and he subsequently acknowledged that he had learned psychoanalysis from them and that his orientation in psychology was to a certain extent an effort to integrate the partial truths he found in their theories. He also often juxtaposed their ideas to those of Freud and defended them from criticism.[14]

When Maslow began his graduate studies in Madison, Wisconsin, he expressed some interest in psychoanalysis. However, the behavioristic orientation of the faculty seems to have eclipsed this interest. In the 1940s Maslow noted that his attitude toward Freud was one of reverence with reservations. He accused Freud and other classical psychoanalysts of studying only half of personality and of being the "worst offenders" in their depiction of human nature. According to Maslow, Freud was mistaken that all behavior is determined by unconscious motives. Rather, Maslow distinguished between neurotic motivation and healthy motivation, the latter being much less directed by unconscious forces. This distinction suggested Maslow's later study of self-actualization in healthy people.[15]

In the 1950s and 1960s, Maslow criticized Freud for his view that the unconscious and regression were unhealthy processes that needed to be controlled and examined. Maslow argued that they could also be sources of creativity, art, love, humor, gaiety, and the like; they could be healthy aspects of personality that should be accepted and nurtured. In the late 1960s, Maslow blamed Freud for studying only the basic needs humans share with the animals and neglecting the "higher human qualities" unique to mankind.[16]

Maslow distinguished between neurotic and non-neurotic motivation. He thought that Freud's mechanisms explained the neurotic personality quite well, but he argued that it was a mistake to extend the conclusions of such studies to generalizations about all humankind. When developing his need-hierarchy theory of human motivation in 1940, Maslow argued that the behavior of healthy persons is much less unconscious than that of neurotics. Healthy behavior, he wrote, is not always directly related to an underlying and ultimately unconscious aim.[17]

As Maslow explored self-actualization and peak-experiences, he argued that Freud was mistaken in describing the unconscious as irrational, dark, and obscure. Id impulses, he suggested, need not be signs of sickness, regression, and enslavement. The unconscious could also be good, beautiful, and desirable. In artistic creation, inspiration, humor, love, and the like, unconscious impulses were indeed revelations of the innermost core of human nature. Growth toward self-actualization, he argued, depends on this essential unconscious core of the person, which needs to be accepted, respected, and loved. One should use the unconscious rather than fear it, accept it rather than control it. In self-actualizing people, Maslow argued, the Freudian id, ego, and superego, the dichotomies of conscious and unconscious, and all internal conflicts are much less sharp than in unhealthy personalities. In peak experiences, for example, these oppositions tend to dissolve. Healthy people have a sense of themselves as conscious, active agents rather than as helpless victims of unconscious forces. Their behavior is understandable without reference to their unconscious life.[18]

Views on Existentialism and Phenomenology

Another important theme in the establishment of humanistic psychology is its relationship with European existential and phenomenological psychology. The founders of humanistic psychology agreed that this idiosyncratic and ill-defined European tradition of thought had an impact in shaping and inspiring humanistic psychology.[19]

It is, however, historically inaccurate to see humanistic psychology as an import of European existentialism. The idea of "parallelism" is more accurate than the "root analogy." In most cases, when humanistic psychologists discovered existentialism in the late 1950s, they had already formulated the core of their psychological thought, although in Maslow, Rogers, and May the reading of Kierkegaard and Buber had a "loosening up effect."[20]

In Maslow we find substantial discussion of existentialism only from the late 1950s on. Maslow was particularly impressed by Martin Buber, but he was also critical of some trends in existentialism, in particular its anti-scientific and anti-biological dimensions. He was as critical of the despairing nihilism (Nietzsche), nothingness (Sartre), and absurdist (Camus) styles of existentialism as he was of behaviorism's S-R philosophy and Freud's psychic determinism. In this sense he was certainly closer to the Kierkegaardian and Buberian brand of existentialism.

Maslow first encountered existentialist ideas in the late 1950s when Adrian Van Kaam, Rollo May, and James Klee introduced him to the literature of existentialism. In the early sixties he already acknowledged that existentialism was a powerful influence in humanistic psychology. With the exception of scarce references to Sartre and Buber, however, he rarely discussed in writing the work of any existentialists. He referred to Sartre as "flat wrong" in his views of human nature. As to Buber, he considered the "I-thou relationship" an example of the emerging humanistic paradigm in psychology.[21]

Although Maslow complained that existentialism was difficult and inaccessible to him, he believed that it would enrich American psychology, even if many existentialist insights merely confirmed existing trends in humanistic psychology. Maslow identified himself with the existentialist interest in the concept of identity and in subjective experiential knowledge.

He praised the existentialists for studying unique characteristics of human nature. He was impressed by their discussion of existential dilemmas, the mystery, paradox, and tragic aspects of life, and the aspirations and limitations of humanity.[22]

After Sartre, Buber was the existentialist thinker most often cited by Maslow. Like Rogers, Maslow thought that Buber's description of the I-Thou relationship constituted a new paradigm in psychotherapy. Following Buber, Maslow argued that the I-thou knowledge that emerges in the experience of deep communication between two people is more valid than the "objective" I-It type of knowledge. The latter, he argued, belongs to the medical paradigm in which the physician treats the patient as an object. The I-Thou paradigm, on the other hand, is based on the intimacy of the encounter between two equal persons and is much more therapeutic.[23]

As to Kierkegaard, Maslow agreed with Rogers' favorite quote from Kierkegaard that the aim of life is "to be that self which one truly is." Like Rogers, Maslow thought that if people are free to grow and to actualize inner potential, they make the right choices. Self-actualizers, argued Maslow, choose what is good for them, primarily because the inner core of their real self is good, trustworthy, and ethical.[24]

Maslow praised the existentialist attack on abstract systems of philosophy that have nothing to do with actual experience. There was no place to turn, Maslow agreed with the existentialists, except the inner self as the source of all validation. In this sense existentialism, so he thought, would supply psychology with the underlying experiential and phenomenological basis it desperately needed.[25]

He often juxtaposed the phenomenological world of the self to the physical world of the scientist and argued that external validation of the positivistic and atomistic type was no more real than the subjective phenomenological world of the experiential self. He believed that phenomenological studies were more truthful to the person, because they focused on how it feels from the internal point of view of the self.[26]

Throughout the 1960s Maslow often rejected what he called Sartrean "arbitrary existentialism." More specifically he addressed Sartre's famous statement that "freedom is existence, and in it existence precedes essence." Sartre argued that there are no essences or reality in human nature. Humans ("being-for-itself") are a "nothingness," a "non-substantial absolute" that exists merely by virtue of the relation toward "being-in-itself." In this sense, argued Sartre, human existence was defined primarily by its freedom and was the result of our "project" in life. Like most humanistic psychologists, Maslow agreed with Sartre that "man is his own project." It is commitment and determination, will and responsibility that make oneself. But he equally thought that Sartre had gone too far in assuming that we are a "nothingness" and that the process of becoming had no biological basis.[27]

He agreed with Sartre that one is ultimately responsible for one's decisions and life project, but he also thought that there is a biological or "instinctoid" basis to human nature. According to Maslow, there is potential in human nature pressing toward actualization, potential that desires by nature to be actualized in the same way that an acorn desires by nature to become an oak tree. These potentialities, however, are dormant and require a culture in order to awaken. "Culture permits or fosters or encourages or helps," wrote Maslow, "what exists in embryo to become real and actual."[28]

Unlike Sartre, Maslow argued that one's life project is not created at random by psychological and life paradoxes but primarily by trends, bents, and tendencies intrinsic to human nature. "To discover" one's nature was for Maslow a much better term than "to create." He thus thought that humanistic psychology was closer to psychodynamics than to Sartre's existentialism. The "uncovering" therapies of the former were meant to help the person to discover true identity rather than to create a self in the Sartrean existentialist sense.[29]

Other Sources of Inspiration

The revolt against behaviorism and psychoanalysis and the inspiration of the neo-Freudians and existentialists were key forces in the making of humanistic psychology. But the founding fathers of humanistic psychology such as Allport, Rogers, and May also found inspiration for the development of their views in Kurt Goldstein, the personality theorists, Gestalt psychology and, to a lesser degree, Eastern thought. Maslow was not an exception.[30]

Maslow met Goldstein in the late 1930s in New York, an event that he recognized many years later as fortunate. In gratitude for this intellectual indebtedness Maslow dedicated *The Psychology of Being* (1962) to Goldstein. According to Maslow, Goldstein influenced two important aspects of his thought: the recognition that the "cool" aspects of Gestalt psychology could be integrated with a more psychodynamic orientation, and the formulation of the holistic-dynamic approach, which stemmed from Goldstein's organismic psychology in that it was holistic, functional, dynamic, and purposive, rather than atomistic, taxonomic, static, and mechanical.[31]

Maslow became well known in psychological circles for his studies on self-actualization. The term "self-actualization," however, was first coined by Goldstein in his studies of brain-injured war veterans. Goldstein employed the concept of self-actualization to explain the reorganization of a person's capacities after injury. According to Goldstein, a damaged organism attempting to survive reorganizes itself into a new unit that incorporates the damages. In this sense the organism is active, generates and recreates itself as it strives toward self-actualization. "Organismic oughtiness" was Maslow's term for this phenomenon.[32]

Maslow acknowledged that he had adopted the concept of "self-actualization" from Goldstein, although he used it in a broader sense. For Maslow "self-actualization" meant the tendency to actualize inner potential. It was the desire to become all one is capable of becoming, to achieve the fullest realization of one's potentialities and intrinsic nature. Like Goldstein, Maslow thought that specific gratification of basic needs helped the individual toward self-actualization.[33]

Maslow carried out a comparative analysis of Goldstein's studies of brain-injured subjects and Skinner's behavioristic psychology, examining in particular the reduction to the concrete and the ability to abstract. The brain-injured do not think in terms of general categories and are unable to integrate separate phenomena into a unity. This phenomenon represents "selective attention" or "obsessional neurosis" at its best, wrote Maslow, comparing it to Skinner's stress on predictability, control, lawfulness, and structure.[34]

Furthermore, Maslow might easily be grouped with the personality theorists. Maslow often complained of lack of emphasis on the study of personality in mainstream psychology. He believed that at the core of the self was a positive growth tendency that strove toward fuller development. If the basic needs are gratified, the self is then released for self-actualization and the gratification of higher needs. This idea would indeed justify including him among the personality theorists.[35]

In regard to Gestalt psychology, Maslow was influenced in the late 1930s by Max Wertheimer and Kurt Koffka at the New School for Social Research in New York. Wertheimer, in particular, had a tremendous impact on Maslow. Wertheimer was described by Maslow as a loving person, almost a parent to Maslow, who allowed him to "hang around" and ask questions. In the prefaces to all of his major publications, Maslow expressed his indebtedness to Gestalt psychology and to Wertheimer in particular.[36]

Maslow emphatically complained that the lessons of Gestalt psychology had not been integrated into mainstream psychology. A person, to the Gestalt psychologists, was an irreducible unit; every aspect of personality was part of an interrelated pattern based on varying relationships within the person and between the person and the environment. Maslow's discussion of the "syndrome"--a complex of symptoms occurring in an organism--in the study of personality in his holistic dynamic theory is a good example of how Gestalt psychologists influenced his thought.[37]

But Maslow was not a mere follower of Gestalt psychology. He emphasized that his health-and-growth psychology represented an attempt to integrate Gestalt theory with the dynamic and functionalist psychologies. In the famous "A Theory of Human Motivation" (1943), for example, Maslow argued that his theory of motivation fused the functionalist tradition with the holism of Gestalt and the dynamism of psychoanalysis.[38]

Eastern thought had a minor influence in the shaping of Maslow's psychology. Maslow first heard of Taoism in Max Wertheimer's seminars at the New School for Social Research. As early as 1949 he used Taoism to describe purposeful spontaneity as an expressive component of behavior. Later he referred to Taoism as synonymous with passivity or resignation in the understanding of nature and the self. He often wrote that Western psychologists should learn from the "taoistic fashion" or "taoistic let-be" or "taoistic listening" when exploring human nature. He meant by this that the scientist should be receptive, trustful, and relaxed and should let things happen without interference in order to attain "experiential knowledge from the inside." He also explored the similarities between the concepts of Satori, Nirvana, peak-experiences, and self-actualization.[39]

In *The Psychology of Science* (1966) Maslow dedicated a chapter to "taoistic science." He described it as an approach to learning meant to complement Western science. He argued that the organization, classification, and conceptualization methods of Western science remove our perception of reality to an abstract realm invented by the mind. This negative aspect of Western science should be balanced against taoistic non-intruding receptivity and contemplation of experience. In one of his last writings he referred to "taoistic objectivity" as opposed to "classical objectivity."[40]

Views on Human Nature

The concept of human nature is the most striking feature of humanistic psychology. Early humanistic psychologists often asserted that any psychology deserving the name entailed a view of human nature. How the question of human nature is approached, they argued, will determine the focus of research, the gathering and interpretation of evidence, and above all the construction of theories. In the long run it was the concept of human nature that served as a common ground and unifying element of the humanistic movement.[41]

Humanistic psychologists shared a conviction that it was the nature of a person to be a "being-in-the-process-of-becoming." At his or her best, they said, a person is proactive, autonomous, choice-oriented, adaptable, and mutable, indeed continuously becoming. To reach the highest levels through the process-of-becoming, a person must be "fully functioning" (Rogers) or "functionally autonomous" (Allport); the self must be spontaneously integrated and actualizing (Maslow); there must be a sense of self-awareness and centeredness (May); there must exist an authenticity-of-being (Bugental). Humanistic psychologists believed that the process-of-becoming was never simply a matter of genetics and biology and they were convinced that the rejection of becoming was a psychological illness that should be the main concern of psychotherapy.[42]

Although they agreed that the process-of-becoming characterizes human nature, humanistic psychologists disagreed regarding the exact causes of that process. Maslow, Rogers, and to a lesser degree Allport, believed that the process-of-becoming had a biological basis. They were nevertheless extremely careful not to revert to simple biological determinism. Maslow thought that humans had an "instinctoid" inner core that contained potentialities pressing toward actualization. Rogers argued that the human organism had a directional and actualizing tendency toward the fulfillment of an inner potential. Bugental and May regarded the biological assumptions of the growth hypothesis as overly vague. They explained the process-of-becoming rather as a product of self-awareness and affirmation--i.e., intentionality--in the face of existential anxiety and contingencies.[43]

Human nature, according to Maslow, depends upon both biology and culture. It seemed obvious to Maslow that there could be no such thing as human nature without the human body. But it seemed equally clear to him that a simple biological determinism could not explain human nature.

Central to Maslow's view of human nature was the concept of an "instinctoid" inner core within the human organism. Innate human capacities, talents, and idiosyncrasies, he thought, have a biological basis in that inner core. However, the biological inner core exists merely as potential "raw material" waiting to be subjectively developed or actualized by the person. The inner core was nothing like an all-powerful animal instinct. It was rather an instinct-remnant, very subtle, both easily suppressed or developed and actualized. There were, according to Maslow, both cultural and psychological dimensions to the process of actualization or suppression. The species-specific potentialities of the human body were, on one hand, shaped by family, education, environment, and culture; on the other hand, they were determined by the person, by his or her choices, will, and decisions, by all those things that Sartre had called the "project."[44]

Since Maslow believed that human biological potential is extremely malleable, he emphasized the importance of a proper cultural environment. A synergetic society, argued Maslow, must create those special conditions that encourage the free expression of instinctoid human nature; more important, it must allow the human organism to actualize itself positively by means of subjective choice. Subjective choice did not mean for Maslow what it meant for Sartrean existentialists. Choices for Maslow were determined by the species-specific biological core residing within the person. The person needed to recognize the impulses (or instinct-remnants) of his or her own body, love and respect his or her own biological organism, then actualize its potential. In spite of the biological foundations of human nature, however, Maslow saw the person as a subjective being responsible for the manner in which he or she individuates and actualizes his or her own existence. Ultimately, it is the person who is the active agent, the mover and chooser, and the master of himself or herself.[45]

Signifying the importance of the person in the unfolding of his or her inner potential, Maslow argued that the inner core developed only by a process of self-discovery and "creation." Although the organism develops from within by virtue of intrinsic growth tendencies, the manner in which this development is accomplished depends upon the person. Maslow agreed with Rogers that there are "positive growth tendencies" that lie within the human organism driving it to fuller-and-fuller development. He also agreed with Rogers that a primary task of psychotherapy is to create an environment conducive to self-discovery and the conscious exercise of will.[46]

Maslow was greatly interested in ethics, and he argued that it was possible to make a scientific study of human values. Values, he thought, were deeply embedded within the structure of human nature, and he believed that the possession of wrong values was a kind of mental illness. Wrong values included the suppression of one's inner biological core, the inhibition of growth, and wanting "what-is-not-good-for-us." Mental health, on the other hand, was synonymous with "good-growth-toward-self-actualization," or the development and actualization to the fullest extent of the capacities latent within the biological core. Maslow considered values leading to self-actualization to be the right values. Actualization is always possible, argued Maslow, because human nature is fundamentally trustworthy, self-governing, and self-protecting. Provided with a synergetic environment and full freedom of self-expression, human nature will unfold and grow in the right direction. Maslow believed that Rogers' ideal of a "fully functioning person" suggested the ethical implications of his own concept of self-actualization.[47]

Maslow's most famous concept was that of a hierarchy of needs. The inner core of human nature, argued Maslow, consists of urges and instinct-like propensities that create basic needs within the person. These needs have to be satisfied; otherwise frustration and sickness will result. The first and most basic needs are physiological and are related to survival. If the physiological needs are not satisfied, all other needs are temporarily pushed aside. Once basic physiological needs are fulfilled, relatively higher needs emerge, such as those for safety, love, and esteem. When safety needs are satisfied, love and esteem needs arise. Social needs stand at the top of Maslow's hierarchy.[48]

According to Maslow, the drive to gratify needs is instinctive; needs must be gratified or illness will ensue. Mental illness is manifested by the person who compulsively seeks gratification of a particular need and does not move on to higher needs. Maslow agreed with Gordon Allport that the satisfaction of higher needs in healthy people is unrelated to the lower needs. Higher needs are independent from lower needs and thus functionally autonomous.[49]

At the top of the hierarchy of needs Maslow placed the need for self-actualization, or the desire to become all that one is capable of becoming. A desire for self-actualization arose with the emergence of a need to know, a need to satisfy our curiosity about nature, a need to understand the perplexities of life; it was also a response to the needs for meaningful work, for responsibility, for justice, for creativity, and for the appreciation of beauty. In *The Farther Reaches of Human Nature* (1971), Maslow discussed a need yet higher than self-actualization, one that was transcendental and centered on cosmic rather than human awareness. All humans, said Maslow, possess an instinctoid need to penetrate the cosmic mysteries and to live in a realm of symbols and religion.[50]

The desire to transcend one's own nature, said Maslow, was just as much an aspect of human nature as were all the lower needs. To deny this ultimate need could be just as pathological as to deny one's need for vitamins and proper nutrition.[51]

In an age when many psychologists understood human nature as a mere response to stimuli, and limited research to the study of psychologically maladjusted persons, Maslow stood for human dignity and humanistic values; he advocated a psychology that studied healthy people, and which trusted and placed the unique potential of each person at the core of its concerns.

ENDNOTES

[1] For a discussion of the place of Maslow in the history of humanistic psychology see Roy J. DeCarvalho, *The Founders of Humanistic Psychology*, (New York: Praeger, 1991). Significant autobiographical references for Abraham Maslow are: *Motivation and Personality* (New York: Harper, 1954), pp. ix; "Two Kinds of Cognition and Their Integration," *General Semantics Bulletin* 20 (1957): 17-22; "Eupsychia-The Good Society," *Journal of Humanistic Psychology* 1 (1961): 1-11; "Lessons From the Peak-Experiences," *Journal of Humanistic Psychology* 2 (1962): 9-18; "A Dialogue With Abraham H. Maslow," *Journal of Humanistic Psychology* 19 (1979): 23-28; *The Farther Reaches of Human Nature* (New York: Viking, 1971), pp. xi-xxi,41,3; "Conversation With Abraham H. Maslow," *Psychology Today* 2 (1968): 34-37,54-57; Willard B. Frick, *Humanistic Psychology: Interviews With Maslow, Murphy and Rogers* (Columbus: Merrill, 1971), pp. 19-49; *Abraham H. Maslow: A Memorial Volume* (Monterey: Brooks/Cole, 1972); R. J. Lowry (Ed.), *The Journals of A. H. Maslow* (Monterey: Brooks/Cole, 1979). For secondary sources see: Edward Hoffman, *The Right To Be Human: A Biography of Abraham Maslow* (Los Angeles: Jeremy Tarcher, 1988); Frank G. Goble, *The Third Force: The Psychology of Abraham Maslow* (New York: Grossman, 1970); Carroll Saussy, *A Study of the Adequacy of Abraham Maslow's Concept of the Self to His Theory of Self-Actualization* (unpublished doctoral dissertation, The Graduate Theological Union, 1977); Richard Grossman, "Some Reflections on Abraham Maslow," *Journal of Humanistic Psychology* 25 (1985): 31-34; *Psychology Today* August 1970, p. 16; Misako Miyamoto, "Professor Abraham H. Maslow (1908-1970)," *Psychologia* 13 (1970): 120; Richard J. Lowry, *A. H. Maslow: An Intellectual Portrait* (Monterey: Brooks/Cole, 1973); Thomas Robert, "Beyond Self-Actualization," *Revision* Winter 1978, pp. 42-46; Colin Wilson, *New Pathways in Psychology: Maslow and the Post-Freudian Revolu-*

tion (London: Gollancz, 1972).

[2] Roy J. DeCarvalho, "A History of the 'Third Force' in Psychology," *Journal of Humanistic Psychology* 30 (1990): 22-44.

[3] DeCarvalho, *The Founders of Humanistic Psychology*, pp. 66-96.

[4] Frick, *Humanistic Psychology*, pp. 19-20. Maslow, *The Psychology of Science* (New York: Harper & Row, 1966), p. 7; "Conversation With Abraham H. Maslow," pp. 37,55.

[5] Maslow's doctoral dissertation was published under different titles in *Journal of Genetic Psychology* 48 (1936): 261-277,278-309; 49 (1936): 161-198; *The Effect of Varying External Conditions on Learning, Retention and Reproduction* (unpublished M.A. thesis, University of Wisconsin-Madison, 1931). Maslow, "Conversation With Abraham H. Maslow."

[6] For the first phase, see Maslow's "Dominance-feeling, Behavior and Status," *Psychological Review* 44 (1937): 404-429; "Dominance, Personality and Social Behavior in Women," *Journal of Social Psychology* 10 (1939): 3-39.

[7] Carl R. Rogers, "The Role of Self-Understanding in the Prediction of Behavior," *Journal of Consulting Psychology* 12 (1948): 174-186; "Some Issues Concerning the Control of Human Behavior," *Science* 124 (1956): 1057-1066. Maslow, *Farther Reaches of Human Nature*, pp. 226-236.

[8] Gordon W. Allport, "Scientific Models and Human Morals," *Psychological Review* ·54 (1947): 182-192; "The Psychologist's Frame of Reference," *Psychological Bulletin* 37 (1940): 1-28; "Fifty Years of Change in American Psychology," *Psychological Bulletin* 37 (1940): 757-776. Maslow, *Motivation and Personality*, pp. 55,63-79,80-100; *The Psychology of Science*, p. 55; "The Farther Reaches of Human Nature," *Journal of Transpersonal Psychology* 1 (1968): 1-9.

[9] DeCarvalho, *The Founders of Humanistic Psychology*, pp. 97-126.

[10] Maslow, *Motivation and Personality*, pp. xiii,66-67,103.

[11] Ibid., p. x; Maslow, *Toward a Psychology of Being* (New York: Nostrand, 1962), p. xi; *The Psychology of Science*, p. xix.

[12] Maslow wrote about New York City in this period as the intellectual

center of the psychological community. See his *Motivation and Personality*, p. ix.

[13] Throughout Maslow's extensive writings, Adler, after Freud, one of the most frequently quoted authors. He referred to Adler at least 77 times. See Jenny Scheele, *Register Referring to the Complete Published Works by A. H. Maslow* (Deft, the Netherlands: Delft University of Technology, 1978), p. 411. See also, Maslow, "Individual Psychology and the Social Behavior of Monkeys and Apes," *International Journal of Individual Psychology* 1 (1935): 47-59; *Motivation and Personality*, pp. x,xi,90-91; "Was Adler a Disciple of Freud? A Note," *Journal of Individual Psychology* 18 (1962): 125. Author's personal correspondence with H. L. Ansbacher of October 29, 1985, and Heinz L. Ansbacher, "Alfred Adler and Humanistic Psychology," *Journal of Humanistic Psychology* 11 (1971): 53-63.

[14] Maslow, *Principles of Abnormal Psychology* (New York: Harper, 1941), pp. xii-xiii; "The Authoritarian Character Structure," *Journal of Social Psychology* 18 (1943): 401-411; *Motivation and Personality*, p. x; "Review of John Schaar, *Escape From Authority, Humanist* 22 (1962): 34-35; *Farther Reaches of Human Nature*, p. xi. Frick, *Humanistic Psychology*, p. 20; Scheele, *Register*, pp. 435,444.

[15] Maslow, "Dominance, Personality and Social Behavior in Women," pp. 4-5; *Motivation and Personality*, pp. 66-67,77-79,90-91,101,193-98.

[16] Maslow, *Toward a Psychology of Being*, pp. 56-57,141-42,182-83,196,60,207-08; *Religion, Values and Peak-Experiences* (Columbus: Ohio State University Press, 1964), pp. 6-8; *The Psychology of Science*, p. 19; "The Farther Reaches of Human Nature," pp. 2-3.

[17] Maslow, "Dominance, Personality and Social Behavior in Women," pp. 4-5; *Motivation and Personality*, pp. 66-67,77,79,90-91,101,193-98.

[18] Maslow, *Toward a Psychology of Being*, pp. 56-57,141-42,182-83,56-57,207-10; *Religion, Values and Peak-Experiences*, pp. 6-8.

[19] DeCarvalho, *The Founders of Humanistic Psychology*, pp. 127-158.

[20] Ibid., pp. 136-138.

[21] Maslow, *Toward a Psychology of Being*, pp. ix,xi.

[22] Maslow explicitly stated his views on existentialism in a paper he presented to the Symposium on Existential Psychology at the 1959 convention of the APA. Rogers and May also presented papers at this symposium. The enthusiastic interest it attracted led Random House to invite Rollo May to edit the papers, which were published in 1961 under the title *Existential Psychology*. Maslow's paper, "Existential Psychology: What's in it For Us?" was also published in *Existential Inquiries*, under the title "Remarks on Existentialism and Psychology," which was reprinted twice, translated into Japanese, and revised for the *Psychology of Being*. In *Eupsychian Management* (Homewood: Irwin-Dorsey, 1965), pp. 127-132, he wrote five additional pages to the original essay. These notes were also reprinted in the *Journal of Humanistic Psychology* 4 (1964): 45-58. See also Maslow, *Toward a Psychology of Being*, pp. 59,174.

[23] Maslow, *Eupsychian Management*, pp. 128-129; *The Psychology of Science*, pp. 52,102-107.

[24] Maslow, *Toward a Psychology of Being*, p. 168; *Farther Reaches of Human Nature*, p. 186.

[25] Maslow, *Toward a Psychology of Being*, pp. 52-60.

[26] Ibid., p. 99; Maslow, *Religion, Values and Peak-Experiences*, pp. 26,41; *The Psychology of Science*, p. 76.

[27] Maslow, *New Knowledge of Human Values* (New York: Harper, 1959), pp. 130-131; *Toward a Psychology of Being*, pp. 167,174-175; *Religion, Values and Peak-Experiences*, p. xvi; *Farther Reaches of Human Nature*, pp. 186,315-316,149; *Motivation and Personality* (New York: Harper & Row, 1954; revised edition, 1970), pp. xvii-xviii. Frick, *Humanistic Psychology*, pp. 22-23.

[28] Ibid.

[29] Ibid.

[30] DeCarvalho, *The Founders of Humanistic Psychology*, pp. 159-178.

[31] Significant references to Goldstein can be found in Maslow's *Principles of Abnormal Psychology*, p. xiii; *Motivation and Personality*, pp. ix, 27,36,80, 89,95,109,116,124,161,166,192,206,262,286,291,296,342,383; *Toward a Psychology of Being*, pp. ii,v,ix,xi,118; *Eupsychian Management*, p. 247; *The Psychology of Science*, pp. 23,42,69; "Conversation With Abraham Maslow," p. 55; *Farther Reaches of Human Nature*, pp. 119,252.

[32] Ibid.

[33] Ibid.

[34] Ibid.

[35] See for example, Maslow, *Motivation and Personality*, p. 116; "Deficiency Motivation and Growth Motivation," in Maurice R. Jones (Ed.) *Nebraska Symposium in Motivation* (Lincoln: University of Nebraska Press, 1955), pp. 1-30; "Personality," in Harry Helso (Ed.) *Theoretical Foundations of Psychology* (New York: Nostrand, 1951), pp. 602-655.

[36] Maslow, *Principles of Abnormal Psychology*, pp. xii,xiii; *Motivation and Personality*, pp. 97,80; "The Authoritarian Character Structure," pp. 31-37; *Toward a Psychology of Being*, p. 215; "A Dialogue With Abraham Maslow," p. 23; *Farther Reaches of Human Nature*, pp. 42,117-119; "Conversation With Abraham Maslow," p. 55. Frick, *Humanistic Psychology*, p. 21.

[37] Ibid.

[38] Ibid.

[39] Maslow, *The Psychology of Science*, p. 96; *Motivation and Personality*, pp. 182,291; "Deficiency Motivation and Growth Motivation," p. 25; *Toward a Psychology of Being*, pp. 55,78,119,136,184; "Lessons from the Peak-Experiences," pp. 12,14,16; *Eupsychian Management*, pp. 6,7,105,154; "A Dialogue with Abraham Maslow," p. 23; *Farther Reaches of Human Nature*, pp. 16-18,115,124,189,191; *Religion, Values and Peak-Experiences*, pp. x,xiii,33,80,100; *The Psychology of Science*, pp. 95-101,124,103.

[40] Ibid.

[41] DeCarvalho, *The Founders of Humanistic Psychology*, pp. 179-182.

[42] Ibid.

[43] Ibid.

[44] Maslow, *Motivation and Personality*, pp. 9,139,382; *Toward a Psychology of Being*, pp. 3-4,138; *Religions, Values and Peak-Experiences*, p. xvi; *Farther Reaches of Human Nature*, pp. 22-24,186.

[45] Maslow, *Motivation and Personality*, pp. 9,124,145,153,349,382; *Farther Reaches of Human Nature*, pp. 101,148,223.

[46] Maslow, *Motivation and Personality*, pp. 116,124; *Toward a Psychology of Being*, p. 138. Frick, *Humanistic Psychology*, pp. 22-24.

[47] Maslow, *Motivation and Personality*, p. 116; *Toward a Psychology of Being*, pp. 167-185,81,130; *Farther Reaches of Human Nature*, pp. 28,211.

[48] Maslow, *Motivation and Personality*, pp. 80,106,116,154,345-347,379-390.

[49] Gordon W. Allport, "A Unique and Open System," *International Encyclopedia of the Social Sciences*, vol. 12, pp. 1-5.

[50] Maslow, *Motivation and Personality*, pp. 183; "Eupsychia-The Good Society," p. 3; *Religion, Values and Peak-Experiences*, p. xvi; "The Farther Reaches of Human Nature"; *Farther Reaches of Human Nature*, p. 186.

[51] Maslow, *Motivation and Personality*, pp. 146-151,379-390; *Toward a Psychology of Being*, p. 222; "The Farther Reaches of Human Nature," p. 3.

Chapter 3

CARL R. ROGERS
AN INTELLECTUAL BIOGRAPHY

Carl Ransom Rogers was born on January 8, 1902, in Chicago, the fourth of six children. His parents were well-educated, upper middle class people with a background in farming. His father was a civil engineer and an independent contractor. His mother was a woman of strong puritan convictions. In his recollections, Rogers wrote that his parents were loving, but also "masters of the art of subtle and loving control," anti-intellectuals, and firm believers in the virtue of work. Characterizing his parents' values as "austere puritanism," he thought that the "gently suppressive atmosphere at home" was the reason he developed an ulcer in his twenties.[1]

Rogers knew how to read before entering grammar school, which he began in the second grade. He enjoyed school activities and read extensively--Bible story books, the encyclopedia, even the dictionary. Throughout adolescence, he had little or no social life outside the family circle; he was withdrawn, dreamy and absent-minded. When he was twelve years old, his family settled in the countryside in order to remove the children from the evil temptations of city life. Rogers enjoyed farm activities, and his interest in high school in scientific agriculture brought him in 1919 to the agriculture program at the University of Wisconsin-Madison. Due to a strong religious inclination, however, he changed majors to history in order to pursue a career in the ministry. Two months after graduating in June 1924 with a B.A. in history, he married and enrolled in the then relatively liberal Union Theological Seminary in New York City, where he was introduced to clinical work. He soon found counseling more congenial than religious work, and began attending courses at Teachers College, Columbia University, where he gained clinical experience with children. In his second year at the seminary, he enrolled full time at Teachers College, where he specialized in clinical and educational psychology, leaving behind the pursuit of a religious career. His doctoral dissertation developed a test for measuring personality adjustment in children.

After graduation in 1928, Rogers joined the Rochester Society for the Prevention of Cruelty to Children in New York State as a child psychologist. He spent the next twelve years performing a wide range of psychological services involving the diagnosis and treatment of delinquent children. In Rochester, Rogers came under the influence of the "relationship therapy" of Otto Rank, Jessie Taft, Frederick Allen, and Virginia Robinson. At this time, he was reluctant to participate in academic psychology because of what he perceived to be its sterility and "rat orientation," as he called it. Rather, he became increasingly involved in the social work profession and clinical and applied psychology. In an attempt to integrate the theory and practice of child guidance with his own experience, he wrote *The Clinical Treatment of the Problem Child* (1939). This work brought him immediate national fame and led to a full professorship at Ohio State University the following year.

In his second year at Ohio, Rogers published *Counseling and Psychotherapy* (1942). This volume was a crystallization of his own clinical work and Rank's relationship therapy. The book focused on the theory and technique of non-directive therapy, the basic tenet of which was that healthy psychological growth occurs when the therapist creates a permissive climate that enables the client to freely express his or her feelings. The therapist must be non-judgmental of the client's feelings and make the client feel free from all coercion or pressure. The theoretical assumption was that such a counseling relationship could lead to self-acceptance and understanding which, in turn, was the first step toward a healthier personality reorientation.

During his Ohio years, Rogers established the first practicum or supervised therapy within a program of academic training in counseling psychology. This practicum was in part responsible for the University of Chicago's invitation to Rogers to establish a counseling center there; an invitation he gladly accepted in 1945. Along with the development of the counseling center at Chicago, Rogers immersed himself in the theoretical formulation of the helping relationship. *Client-Centered Therapy* (1951) was a product of this interest. In this work, Rogers abandoned the term "non-directive" for the term "client-centered," thus alluding to a theoretical shift. He thought that the individual has a drive toward growth, health, and adjustment. In this context, therapy was viewed as a matter of freeing the person for normal growth or self-actualization.

Rogers argued that a constructive change in personality and behavior is possible if certain basic conditions are experienced by the client in the counseling relationship. These "necessary and sufficient conditions of therapeutic personality change" are: (1) the realness and congruence of the therapist; (2) unconditional positive regard; and (3) empathic understanding of the client's situation. No special intellectual or professional knowledge is essential in this process, since the focus is deliberately on the feeling aspects of the immediate situation rather than upon the intellectual aspects.

In 1957, Rogers accepted an appointment in psychiatry and psychology at the University of Wisconsin-Madison in psychiatry and psychology to study psychotic individuals. Rogers hoped to use his position to try to influence the training of psychiatrists. But he encountered resistance from departments that were heavily experimental, "rat-oriented," distrustful of clinical psychology, and skeptical of his views. Deeply disappointed with what he considered to be the antiquated and primitive structure of graduate education in psy-

chology at Wisconsin, he resigned from the psychology department. He re-
tained, however, the appointment in psychiatry, and continued to research
the impact of the client-centered therapeutic relationship upon schizophrenic
patients. With the problems in the organization of the research staff and the
antagonism of the psychology faculty, Rogers characterized the Wisconsin
years as the most painful and anguished of his professional life.[2] *The Therapeutic Relationship and Its Impact* (1967) presented the conclusions of Rogers' and his associates on the efficacy of psychotherapy in treating schizophrenics.

Rogers presented further theoretical developments in client-centered
therapy in *On Becoming a Person* (1961). In this work, he elaborated on the
notion that the human organism has an "actualizing tendency" to develop all
its capacities in order to maintain or enhance its existence. Applying this
insight to psychotherapy, Rogers argued that the task of the therapist is to
release this organismic capacity in order to induce growth and psychological
well-being. In this context, he thought that individuals have the capacity to
penetrate their own complexities if they are only given a suitable psychological climate. The client is ultimately the expert in dealing with his or her own
feelings and life situation. The function of the therapist is merely a facilitative one.

Disappointed with the antagonism and skepticism toward his views at
Madison and in education in general, Rogers resigned and moved to the
Western Behavioral Sciences Institute (WBSI) in California, a nonprofit
organization which was devoted to humanistic research in interpersonal relationships. At WBSI, among a congenial interdisciplinary group and free from
bureaucratic entanglement, Rogers turned to research on the experience of
normal individuals in encounter groups. The result was *Encounter Groups*
(1970). During this period, Rogers was also involved in educational projects.
Disappointed with the educational system at Madison, he linked his experience with encounter groups to education. In *Freedom to Learn* (1969),

Rogers tried to show how educators could facilitate learning even within an antiquated and fossilized system by being personal and innovative. In his two other publications, *Becoming Partners* (1972) and *Carl Rogers on Personal Power* (1977), Rogers explored intimate relationships and political realities in the context of his overall thinking.

After leaving WBSI, Rogers worked at the Center for the Studies of the Person. He considered the Center to be a "pilot study" for the organization of the future. It was a loosely organized group of 45 people that offered, among other things, training programs for encounter group facilitators.

In the late 1970s, Rogers developed an interest in psychic and paranormal phenomena, such as altered states of mind and phenomena not perceptible by the five senses. He read the psychic, Carlos Castaneda, for example. After the death of his wife, Rogers held a spiritualist seance with a medium to attempt to contact the surviving soul of Helen. Rogers considered the seance a success. He came to believe that the human soul is a spiritual essence that lasts over time and occasionally incarnates in a human body.[3]

Despite advanced age, Rogers remained active until his death in February, 1987. During his last years, he explored the application of encounter group techniques to the solution of international conflicts in Central America, South Africa, Northern Ireland, and the Soviet Union.

Views on Behavioristic Psychology

The humanistic psychology advocated by the founding members of the Association for Humanistic Psychology and its leading representatives, Gordon Allport, Abraham Maslow, Carl Rogers, Rollo May, and James Bugental, was an outcry against what they regarded as the academic sterility of behaviorism and its mechanistic concept of human nature. Thus the writing of the humanistic psychologists often contrasted behavioristic and humanistic interpretations of human nature, psychotherapy, method and ethics.

Rogers, like Maslow, was not an exception.[4]

Rogers' lifelong critique of behaviorism was highlighted by his public debate with Skinner in the 1950s and 1960s on freedom and the control of human behavior. In the 1940s and early 1950s, Rogers published enough critical remarks about behaviorism to attract the attention of Skinner himself, who in reply invited Rogers to a friendly public debate at the American Psychological Association meeting of 1956. The purpose of the debate was to clarify the divergent trends they represented regarding the use of scientific knowledge in the control of human behavior. Skinner's position, with which Rogers totally disagreed, was that psychologists should use their power to assume control of human affairs. The debate stirred the emotions of the large audience. Rogers expressed dissatisfaction mainly because the argument was of the either-or type.[5]

Rogers again encountered Skinner when the latter presented a paper four years later to the American Academy of Arts and Sciences on the subject of the individual and the design of cultures. During the next two years, Rogers continued to write critiques of Skinner and behaviorism in general.[6]

Both Skinner and Rogers felt they were touching an important nerve in American culture, and so another debate was organized in the summer of 1962 in Duluth, Minnesota. The resulting nine-hour confrontation attracted an audience of nine hundred people. Rogers recognized later that this debate had been the most thorough exploration yet held on the conflict between humanistic psychology and behaviorism concerning education and the control of human behavior. Later, he complained that the tape of the dialogue was intended to have been made public but that Skinner was reluctant to give his permission. Feeling the "profession was cheated," Rogers called Skinner's attitude "needlessly fearful." Many years afterwards, Skinner replied that he had not given permission for the release of the tapes because he did not want them to circulate without editing his portion; he also complained about the poor quality of the recording. The tapes were released to the public in 1976, when the confrontation and the issues involved had been largely forgotten.[7]

The last public encounter between Rogers and Skinner took place in a symposium on phenomenology and behaviorism in 1963 at Rice University that attracted considerable attention both within and outside psychological circles. Rogers' lecture was philosophical. He discussed at some length the experimental, phenomenological and humanistic views of human nature, the question of scientific method, and attempted to accommodate subjective and objective philosophies of science. Much later, Rogers thought that this presentation was a new direction in his thinking and work.[8]

Rogers' last critique of Skinner took place in 1964. Rogers, who had been elected "humanist of the year" that year by the American Humanistic Association, criticized Skinner's philosophy of social control. In his address on "Freedom and Commitment" to the American Psychological Association, Rogers contrasted the humanistic meaning of freedom with Skinner's views. It has been suggested that Skinner's *Beyond Freedom and Destiny* (1971) was an answer to Rogers' critique.[9]

For the behaviorist, so maintained Rogers, a person was an inanimate, purely reactive organism, a passive helpless thing not responsible for its own behavior: indeed, a nothing but a response to stimuli and a mere collection of independent habits. In his critique, Rogers argued that human motivation is instead purposive, choice-oriented, and autonomous. Individuals have subjective values that provide guidance and direction to life. An understanding of such intentional attitudes and motives, he argued, is a prerequisite to understanding behavior and human nature.

Like most humanistic psychologists, Rogers criticized Skinner's belief that behavior was the result of environmental reinforcement, planned or unplanned. Rogers and Skinner had agreed to an advance exchange of manuscripts before the APA debate of 1956. Skinner used the word "choice" several times in his first draft; when Rogers returned the manuscript to Skinner, he commented that Skinner's use of the word "choice" contradicted

a belief in strict environmental determinism. In reply, Skinner carefully elimi-
nated, replaced or put in quotes the word choice. In the final presentation of
the papers, Rogers noted the alteration and stated that "Skinner had dropped
all notions that the individual makes any value choices for himself."[10]

Four years later when Rogers attended Skinner's lecture on the subject
of the individual and the design of culture, Rogers asked Skinner if he
thought it was an illusion that he had chosen to come to the lecture, that he
had a purpose for the meeting, and that he existed as a person. Rogers
remarked that "he [Skinner] actually made certain marks on a paper and
emitted certain sounds here simply because his genetic make-up and his past
environment had operantly conditioned his behavior in such a way that it was
rewarding to make these sounds and that he, as a person, doesn't enter into
this." Skinner answered that he did not want to deal with the question of
whether he had any choice in the matter, since this was a philosophical, not a
scientific, problem. But Skinner did accept Rogers' characterization of his
presence in the room. As opposed to Skinner's environmental determinism,
Rogers argued that people have the capacity to make significant subjective
appraisals, choices, and decisions.[11]

In the discussion with Skinner, Rogers was particularly critical of the
behavioristic contention that since people do not have the capacity for self-
understanding and self-direction they should rely on experts for measurement, evaluation, and guidance. Science, in this sense, thought Rogers, transforms people into objects that can be measured and regulated, thereby
weakening, degrading, and even eliminating one's opportunity for becoming
oneself through a process of responsible decisions. Rogers thought that this
idea was threatening because the evaluation of the experts brings management and manipulation of the many by the self-selected few. Rogers saw
potential danger if tools of behavioral control fell into the hands of a totali-
tarian regime. Rogers argued that any discussion of behavioral control must
first deal with the questions: Who will control? What type of control to use?

Toward what end, purpose, or value the control? These questions raise the issues of purpose and values that are extrinsic to science itself. According to Rogers, even perfect random experimentation is a value choice. In other words, Rogers argued that there is purpose and choice in human action, exactly what Skinner had emphatically denied.[12]

In the context of the discussion over control and prediction of behavior, Rogers compared the ability to predict behavior by means of external scientific control of the behavioristic type with that of internal self-knowledge posited by humanistic science. He argued that people resent and rebel against external scientific control, but they accept the increase of self-knowledge that allows them to control their own behavior. Self-knowledge of the humanistic type has in this sense much more predictive power. Maslow made an identical argument.[13]

Rogers summarized the differences between behaviorism and humanistic psychology as an extra-scientific problem based on the individual's "philosophical choice" concerning their understanding of human nature. He argued that behavioristic and humanistic psychologists have concluded, even before looking at the data, whether people are reactive or proactive. Once this philosophical choice has been made, consciously or not, the paths of study would continue to diverge.[14]

Views on Psychoanalysis

As previously noted, humanistic psychologists have described their approach as a "third force" in psychology, after behaviorism and psychoanalysis. Rogers, like Maslow, counterposed his views to classical Freudian psychoanalysis, developing the argument that humanistic psychology was in a sense an antidote, not only to behaviorism but also to the formalism, determinism, and dogma of psychoanalysis. Also like Maslow, Rogers paid a somewhat ambivalent tribute to Freud by describing the broader phenomenological and existential conception of human nature contained in humanistic psychology as complementing rather than replacing Freud's observations.[15]

In considering the impact of the psychoanalytic school on Rogers and humanistic psychology in general, however, a distinction must be made between Freud--or classical psychoanalytical thought--and the neo-Freudians. Although in general humanistic psychologists paid homage to Freud, they also often criticized Freud's psychoanalytical interpretation of human nature. Their views toward the neo-Freudians, however, were less ambivalent. Alfred Adler, Erik Fromm and Karen Horney, for example, were a major influence on Rollo May and Maslow.[16]

Otto Rank was the most influential figure of the psychoanalytical movement who had a significant impact on Rogers during the formative period of client-centered therapy. During the 1930's when Rogers was in Rochester, New York, some of the social workers there had taken courses at the Pennsylvania School of Social Work that followed the orientation of Rank. Their enthusiasm about Rank's new "relationship therapy" led Rogers to invite Rank to Rochester for a weekend. Rogers was impressed with Rank's description of therapy, particularly with his emphasis on the importance of listening to the feelings behind the client's words and of "reflecting" them back to the client. Moreover, Rank's claim that the person has potential for growth and that therapy should rely on human qualities rather than on intellectual skills proved to be, wrote Rogers, an effective way of working with people in distress. Rogers' first publications, including *The Clinical Treatment of the Problem Child* (1939), became increasingly critical of classical Freudian psychoanalysis and sympathetic to "relationship" or "passive" therapy as advanced by Rank.[17]

When Rogers was asked in 1975 to comment on Freud's views, he answered that they all contained a germ of truth. Rogers often praised Freud as a very flexible researcher who changed, altered, and revised his terminology according to his own clinical experience. It was in the hands of his followers, thought Rogers, that Freud's psychoanalysis deteriorated into a narrow and dogmatic orthodoxy comparable to religious fundamentalism.[18]

Rogers first encountered psychoanalysis in his mid-twenties at the Institute for Child Guidance in New York City, where he fulfilled the internship requirement for the doctorate degree from Teachers College, Columbia University. Rogers remembered that at Teachers College Freud's name was considered a "dirty word." The approach at Teachers College was rigorous and scientific. But at the Institute for Child Guidance, Rogers observed that he "soaked up the dynamic Freudian view of the staff." Rogers' first clinical treatment of a child in the Institute was based almost exclusively on psycho-analytical theories.[19]

Rogers criticized classical psychoanalysis on therapeutic grounds. As early as the 1940s, Rogers focused his critique on those psychoanalytical procedures which required "assimilated intellectual interpretation." He argued that classical psychoanalytical therapy was over-intellectualized in that it aimed to change patient attitudes through the patient's assimilation of an intellectual interpretation of his or her own behavior. But an intellectualized interpretation of behavior, argued Rogers, cannot itself alter behavior no matter how accurate that interpretation may be. Self-understanding is achieved inwardly; it is emotional, not rational, and it cannot be imposed. Rogers believed that "resistance" to the therapist was not an inevitable consequence of the therapy, but took place when the therapist confronted the client too rapidly with a highly intellectualized explanation.[20]

Client-centered therapy, Rogers stated, aimed at greater independence and self-interpretation on the part of the individual than did classical psychoanalysis. It aimed at helping the client solve his or her own problems efficiently and without need of a therapist. There was more emphasis in client-centered therapy on the emotional and immediate situation than on personality reorganization through the intellectualization of the client's past experiences.[21]

As Rogers' thoughts on therapy matured, he criticized classical psychoanalysis in terms of his distinction between directive and non-directive therapy. Rogers argued that traditional psychoanalysts believed that they must control the therapeutic relationship because they had no confidence in the client's own capacity to achieve self-understanding. Client-centered therapy took the opposite approach: the therapist should trust the capacity of the individual for self-understanding in the therapeutic setting.[22]

Rogers also criticized the Freudian concept of "transference." Therapeutic improvement is more rapid and efficient, he argued, if the client's emotional transference of attitudes to the therapist is openly expressed and accepted by the therapist with "unconditional positive regard." Then the client will eventually understand that transference has taken place, thereby dissolving that transference. The transference should not be discussed with the client before he or she consciously experiences the transference attitudes; otherwise the client will resist the transference explanation.[23]

In his mature writings, Rogers' criticism of Freud focused primarily on Freud's understanding of human nature. He argued that Freud's assessment of human nature was overly pessimistic, too fatalistic, too deterministic; Freud, he said, focused too exclusively on the dark side of human nature, not taking into account an individual's sense of personhood, freedom, and dignity. Rogers believed that Freud accepted the need for control, both in society and personality, mainly because Freud considered the individual to be "innately destructive," irrational, and unsocial. Rogers understood Freud to mean that destruction, incest, murder, and other crimes would follow if one's real human nature were allowed free expression. Freud erred, said Rogers, by believing that a person's entire life is merely a reaction to early childhood fixations, castration threats, and Oedipal fantasies. It was as if an individual was forever a prisoner who could not escape the primitive passions which originated in these fixations. He argued that Freud considered personality to be the "willy-nilly" product of powerful and unrestrained biological drives.

According to Freud, he said, a person can direct but can never transform the id's basic structure. Freudian personality dynamics could thus do no more than restrain the forces of the id, seeking either their sublimation or equilibrium.[24]

Views on Existentialism and Phenomenology

Another important theme in the intellectual history of humanistic psychology is its relationship with European existential and phenomenological psychology. This European intellectual tradition had an important impact in shaping humanistic psychology and remains an important stream within this psychological discipline.[25]

The Cincinnati Symposium on existential psychology organized by Rollo May at the APA meeting of 1959 and the publication of the papers that followed were significant events that cemented identification of Rogers, Maslow, May, and Allport with an American brand of existential psychology. It was only in the mid-1960s that this home-grown existentialism was labeled humanistic psychology.[26]

Whereas during the 1940s Rogers was under the influence of Rank, in the late 1950s the ideas of Kierkegaard and Buber held sway. In the early 1950s, Rogers was increasingly divided between the tenets of logical positivism and of subjectivism. Some theology students at Chicago had persuaded him to read the basic writings of Buber and Kierkegaard. Kierkegaard had a "loosening up" effect upon Rogers, encouraging him to trust and to express his own experience. He thought that Kierkegaard's insights and convictions expressed views he had held, but was unable to formulate. One of these insights was found in a passage from *The Sickness Unto Death* (1954), in which Kierkegaard argued that the aim of life is "to be that self which one truly is." Rogers interpreted the passage to mean that the most common despair results from not being responsible for becoming what one truly wants to be, but rather desiring to be something else. This idea was, indeed, a cornerstone of Rogers' thought on the self and on therapy.[27]

   Rogers, like Kierkegaard, thought that the goal of life was to move away from "oughts" and facades. But, while the goal of Kierkegaard was to purify Christianity, Rogers rather addressed issues of psychotherapy. In therapy, argued Rogers, when the individual becomes what he is inwardly, he is able to hear the inner messages and meanings of the self. When this happens, a deep desire to be fully oneself in all one's complexity and richness follows, withholding and fearing nothing that is part of the inner self. Self-experience becomes a friendly resource and not a frightening enemy. If the conditions that promote growth in psychotherapy are present (such as unconditional positive regard, empathic understanding, and self-understanding), the choices of the individual will be true to his or her nature. Psychotherapy makes it possible for the person to consider choices with greater objectivity and select those that promote a healthy biological and psychic growth. The task of the therapist is merely to form an alliance with the natural forces of the individual. In Rogers' understanding, this was exactly what Kierkegaard intended in his philosophical writings.[28]

   The theology students in Chicago also introduced Rogers to the thinking of the Hasidic philosopher, Martin Buber. Between 1953 and 1960, Rogers wrote extensively on the psychotherapeutic significance of the therapist as a person. He thought that, in addition to "unconditional positive regard," and the immediacy and realness of the therapist, a deep sense of communication and unity between therapist and client was crucial. In this sense, therapy was a genuine person-to-person experience. This was exactly what Buber had described in the "I-thou relationship." Buber thought that the deep mutual experience of speaking truly to another without playing a "role," or the meeting between two persons at a deep and significant level, had a healing effect. Buber named this process "healing through meeting." It was a process Rogers argued to have had experienced in the most effective moments of psychotherapy.[29]

But Rogers was also at times critical of some trends in existentialism. The most persistent critique, and one he addressed specifically to Sartre, focused on Sartre's statement that "freedom is existence, and in it existence precedes essence." Sartre had argued that there are no essences in human nature. There is no inner structure or reality that defines human nature. Human existence is a "nothingness," a "non-substantial absolute" or "being-for-itself," which exists merely by virtue of its relation to "being-in-itself." In this sense, argued Sartre, human existence was defined primarily by its freedom and was the result of our "project" in life. Rogers agreed with Sartre that "man is his project." It is commitment and determination, will and responsibility that make oneself. But he equally thought that Sartre had gone too far in assuming that we are a "nothingness" and that the process of becoming has no biological basis.[30]

Unlike Sartre, Rogers rather emphasized the biological basis of the process of becoming. In the late 1970s, Rogers explained this belief as the "actualizing tendency of organic life," and "the organismic tendency towards fulfillment." Like Maslow and Allport, Rogers also spoke of the process of therapy as a process of "discovering" a settled inner biological self. According to Rogers, humans, like animals, are organisms that develop or grow according to the dictates of innate qualities. What is different in the human species, he argued, is that at a certain point in the biological development, consciousness arises and changes everything.[31]

He thought that there is a biological core or essence in human nature that precedes existence, exactly what Sartre denied. Rogers also found the Sartrean brand of existentialism to be overly pessimistic. He believed that his humanistic brand of existentialism provided more hope and optimism in confronting the mystery, anguish, and despair of life. Not surprisingly Rogers once referred to the "despairing existentialists." In his opinion humanistic psychology was more positive in its view of human nature and closer to

Kierkegaard and Buber than to radical French existentialism; a phenomenon Rogers attributed to the fact that, as a nation, Americans had been more fortunate than the French, since they had not suffered two world wars fought on their homeland.[32]

As to the classical studies of European phenomenologists, we find little discussion in Rogers' writings. Rogers understood phenomenology as a method opposed to the causological approach of the physical sciences based on observation and description, and aimed at the study of subjective reports of immediate experience and of introspective nature. It was in this sense, according to Rogers, that client-centered therapy was phenomenological. Throughout the 1950s, he advocated the Q-technique developed by his colleague William Stephenson for the "objective analysis of phenomenological data." The Q-technique aimed to treat objectively the complex data drawn from the internal frame of reference of the individual. The classical European phenomenologists, however, would certainly dispute Rogers' definition of phenomenology.[33]

Other Sources of Inspiration

    ˙   The revolt against behaviorism and psychoanalysis and the inspiration of the neo-Freudians and existentialists were the key forces in the making of humanistic psychology. But the founders of humanistic psychology, such as Allport, Maslow, May--and Rogers--also found inspiration in Kurt Goldstein, the personality theorists, Gestalt psychology, and, to a lesser degree, Eastern thought.[34]

Rogers acknowledged that his thought on the process of therapy had been influenced by Goldstein's organismic psychology. He wrote that Goldstein had enriched his thinking, citing in particular the "actualizing tendency" or "growth hypothesis." While Goldstein argued that the drive to self-actualization impels the organism of the brain-injured war veteran to actualize itself in different areas, Rogers quite similarly argued that the motivating construct of effective therapy relied in great part on the actualizing or growth tendency of the patient.[35]

Rogers' emphasis on the study of the self as a process of becoming undoubtedly places him among the personality theorists. His statements on personality dynamics and behavior in the chapter on "A Theory of Personality and Behavior" in *Client-Centered Therapy* (1951) is the earliest evidence of his interest in the study of personality. Rogers employed the terminology of personality theorists in writing that the "internal frame of reference" of the individual was the best way to understand the self. He concluded that his theory of personality "relies heavily upon the concept of the self as an explanatory construct." Rogers' emphasis on the self and personality theory permeates most of his publications and was duly emphasized in several encyclopedia essays on client-centered therapy written in the 1970s.[36]

George Kelly was the personality theorist whom Rogers referred to most often in his writings. Kelly had been Rogers' colleague at Ohio State University. In 1956, Rogers reviewed Kelly's *Psychology of Personal Constructs* for the periodical *Contemporary Psychology*, praising it lavishly as "highly rewarding reading." The most original and valuable section of the book, wrote Rogers, was on the psychology of personal constructs, a theory Rogers himself occasionally employed to clarify issues in client-centered therapy.[37]

There were also points of contact between Gestalt psychology and the thought of Rogers--"parallels rather than roots," in Rogers' own words--and he referred, in particular, to the Gestalt psychology advocated by Kurt Lewin. As early as 1947, when Rogers became conscious of the theoretical implications of client-centered therapy, he realized that, like Lewin, he employed a field theory. Both aimed to study the individual at the present moment, not in the sense of historical development or genetic determination. Rogers' assumption that the experience of the present field determines behavior was,

according to Rogers, related to the Gestalt psychology of Kurt Lewin. Rogers
pointed to this relationship between perception and behavior by rephrasing
Lewin's comment that behavior is primarily a reaction to "reality-as-perceived." He pointed out that alterations in the perception of the self also
alters behavior.[38]

Views on Human Nature

One of the distinguishing characteristics of humanistic psychology in
the late 1960s was its view of human nature. Humanistic psychologists,
Rogers among them, argued that the question of human nature determines
the focus of research, the gathering and interpretation of evidence, and
above all, the construction of psychological theories. Most humanistic psychologists, including Maslow and Rogers, thus devoted great effort in delineating a view of human nature. In the long run, it was the concept of human
nature that became the common ground and unifying element of the humanistic movement.[39]

Humanistic psychologists shared a conviction that a person is a "being-
in-the-process-of-becoming." At its best, they said, a person is proactive,
autonomous, choice-oriented, adaptable, and mutable, indeed, continuously
becoming. Each human being, they argued, is a unique organism with the
ability to direct, choose, and change the guiding motives or "project" of life's
course. Humanistic psychologists believed that the process-of-becoming was
never simply a matter of genetics and biology and they were convinced that
the rejection of becoming was a psychological illness that should be the main
concern of psychotherapy.[40] Describing human nature in terms of growth and
development, they argued that this process must be understood in both
biological and non-biological terms. Rogers' views on human nature illustrated both of these propensities. According to Rogers, the unfolding of an
organism's potential is a process largely determined by genetics; what sepa-

rates human beings from the rest of nature, he maintained, was the development of consciousness.

Rogers placed his view of development within a broad evolutionary context which was, though distinct, reminiscent of the evolutionary systems of Lamarck and Herbert Spencer in the nineteenth century. Rogers thought that a "formative directional tendency" permeates all beings in the universe, from crystals to stellar space and organic life. He saw this directional tendency within evolutionary terms as the development toward greater complexity, interrelatedness, and order. In living organisms, the directional tendency, he said, becomes an "actualizing tendency." All organisms desire to maintain, enhance, and reproduce themselves; they also desire to gain independence from external control, to become self-regulated, and even to transcend their own nature. Although the actualizing tendency can be inhibited by an adverse environment, Rogers believed that it can never be destroyed so long as the organism is alive. Rogers agreed with Maslow that certain lower conditions must be fulfilled before higher needs emerge to press the organism toward further actualization. Like Allport, he also believed that actualization is relatively independent of antecedent needs.[41]

The actualizing tendency does not, however, involve the development of all the potentials within the organism. It is selective and directive only toward positive objectives; it does not, for example, actualize the capacity for nausea, self-destruction or the ability to bear pain.[42]

Rogers believed that there is a biological base to human nature. At a certain point in evolution, however, the formative tendency of the human organism achieved consciousness of itself. According to Rogers, consciousness created a "symbolizing capacity, topping a vast pyramid of nonconscious organismic functioning." To be conscious, said Rogers, meant to be aware of one's own growth and development. Consciousness on its turn introduced the ability to understand one's inner self. If an individual makes choices that are in tune with his or her own organism, Rogers argued, these could be called good choices. These were, however, not "objective" or "real" choices since they were ultimately determined by the subjective actualizing tendency, which Rogers described as a kind of "automatic pilot."[43]

Rogers considered a "fully functioning person" to be one who is in touch with his or her own inner nature; one who trusts and allows his or her own organism to function freely; and one who selects from among all the organismic potentialities what is most genuinely satisfying. "The basic nature of the human being," wrote Rogers, "when functioning freely is constructive and trustworthy."[44]

Rogers made the actualizing tendency the central hypothesis of his person-centered approach to psychotherapy. He believed that people can learn to tap their own actualizing tendency and fulfill their inner potential if they are surrounded by a "definable climate" of facilitative attitudes. The task of psychotherapy was thus to facilitate self-understanding in the hope that it will allow the individual to direct his or her own life in constructive and fulfilling ways according to the dictates of their own organism.[45]

In an age when many psychologists understood human nature as a mere response to stimuli, Carl Rogers stood for human dignity and values, advocating a humanistic psychology that trusted the unique potential of each human being.

ENDNOTES

[1] Rogers' significant autobiographical references are: *Becoming a Person* (Boston: Houghton Mifflin, 1961); "Freedom and Commitment, *The Humanist* 24 (1964): 37-40; "Autobiography," in E. W. Boring & G. Lindzey (Eds.), *A History of Psychology in Autobiography* (New York: Appleton-Century-Crofts); "Interview-a," *Psychology Today* 1 (1967): 19-21,62-66; "Interview-b," in W. B. Frick (Ed.), *Humanistic Psychology: Interviews with Maslow, Murphy and Rogers* (Columbus: Merrill, 1971); "My Philosophy of Interpersonal Relationships and How it Grew," *Journal of Humanistic Psychology* 13 (1973): 3-15. Significant biographical sources are, "American

Psychological Association-Award for Distinguishing Professional Contributions: 1972," *American Psychologist* 28 (1973): 71-74; Richard I. Evans, *Carl Rogers: The Man and His Ideas* (New York: Dutton, 1975); Howard Kirschenbaum, *On Becoming Carl Rogers* (New York: Delacorte, 1979); Andre dePeretti, *Pensee et Verite de Carl Rogers* (Toulouse: Privat, 1974).

[2] Rogers, "Autobiography," p. 371.

[3] Rogers, *A Way of Being* (Boston: Houghton Mifflin, 1980), pp. 91-92.

[4] Roy J. DeCarvalho, *The Founders of Humanistic Psychology* (New York: Praeger, 1991), chap. 4. Rogers, "Some Questions and Challenges Facing a Humanistic Psychology," *Journal of Humanistic Psychology* 5 (1965): 1-5; "Comments on Pitt's Article," *Journal of Humanistic Psychology* 13 (1973): 83-84; Evans, *Rogers*, pp. 115,130-35.

[5] Rogers, "Divergent Trends in Methods of Improving Adjustment," *Pastoral Psychology* 3 (1948): 11-40; "A Personal View of Some Issues Facing Psychologists," *American Psychologist* 10 (1955): 247-249; "Persons or Questions," *Cross Currents* 3 (1955): 289-306; "Implications of Recent Advances in the Prediction and Control of Behavior," *Teachers College Record* 57 (1956): 316-322; *On Becoming a Person*, pp. 363-64.

[6] Rogers, "Client-centered Therapy," in E. Arieti, *American Handbook of Psychiatry* (New York: Basic Books), p. 197; "Significant Learning in Therapy and in Education," *Educational Leadership* 16 (1959): 232-242; *On Becoming a Person*, pp. ix,363-364, chaps. 20-21; "In Retrospect," in Evans, *Rogers*, p. 132.

[7] Rogers, "Some Thoughts Regarding the Current Philosophy of the Behavioral Sciences," *Journal of Humanistic Psychology* 5 (1965): 182-194; "Interview-b," p. 62; "In Retrospect," p. 130; G. Gladstein, *A Dialogue on Education and the Control of Human Behavior* (An audio-cassette) (New York: Norton, 1976).

[8] Rogers, "Toward a Science of the Person," *Journal of Humanistic Psychology* 5 (1965): 182-194; T. W. Wann, *Behaviorism and Phenomenology* (Chicago: University of Chicago Press, 1964).

[9] Rogers, "Freedom and Commitment"; Evans, *Rogers*, p. 114.

[10] Rogers, "Comments on Pitt's Article," p. 83; "Some Issues Concern-

ing the Control of Human Behavior," in Evans, *Rogers*, pp. xiiv-lxxxviii; "Foreword & Conversation," in J. T. Hart & T. M. Tomlinson (Eds.), *New Directions in Client-centered Therapy* (Boston: Houghton Mifflin, 1970), pp. 521-523; "An Encounter with Carl Rogers," *Res Publica* (Claremont Men's College), 1 (1973): 41-51; "Interview on Growth," in W. Oltmans (Ed.), *On Growth* (New York: Putman's Sons, 1974), pp. 197-205; *Carl Rogers On Personal Power* (New York: Delacorte, 1977), p. 19.

[11] Rogers, "Comment," *Journal of Counseling Psychology* 9 (1962): 16-17; "Learning to be Free," in S. M. Farber & R. H. Wilson (Eds.), *Conflict and Creativity* (New York: McGraw-Hill, 1963), pp. 268-288; "In Retrospect," p. 132.

[12] Rogers, "Some Issues"; "A Personal View"; "Freedom and Commitment"; "Divergent Trends," pp. 13,18; "Persons or Science," p. 298; "Implications of Recent Advances," pp. 318-321.

[13] Rogers, "The Role of Self-understanding in the Prediction and Control of Behavior," *Journal of Consulting Psychology* 12 (1948): 174-186; "Some Issues," p. lxiii. A. H. Maslow, *The Psychology of Science* (New York: Harper, 1966), pp. 40-44.

[14] Rogers, "Comments on Pitt's Article," p. 83; Evans, *Rogers*, pp. 115,130-135.

[15] Rogers, "Three Surveys of Treatment Measures Used With Children," *American Journal of Orthopsychiatry* 7 (1937): 48-57; *Client-Centered Therapy* (Boston: Houghton Mifflin, 1951), p. 4; *On Becoming a Person*, p. 32; "Toward a Science," p. 72.

[16] R. J. DeCarvalho, *The Founders*, chap. 7.

[17] Rogers, "The Clinical Psychologist's Approach to Personality Problems," *The Family* 18 (1937): 233-143; "Three Surveys," p. 56; *The Clinical Treatment of the Problem Child* (Boston: Houghton Mifflin, 1939), pp. 338,346; *Becoming a Person*, p. 9; "Autobiography," pp. 356,360; "Person-Centered Personality Theory," in R. Corsini (Ed.), *Current Personality Theories* (Itasca: Peacock, 1973), p. 128.

[18] Rogers, "A Theory of Therapy, Personality, and Interpersonal Relationships, as Developed in the Client-Centered Framework," in S. Koch (Ed.), *Psychology: A Study of a Science* (New York: McGraw-Hill, 1959), pp.

184-256; *On Becoming a Person*, p. ix; Evans, *Rogers*, pp. 6-8,88-89.

[19] Rogers, "The Processes of Therapy," *Journal of Consulting Psychology* 4 (1940): 161-164; *On Becoming a Person*, p. 9; "Autobiography," p. 356.

[20] Rogers, "The Process of Therapy," p. 163; *Counseling and Psychotherapy* (Boston: Houghton Mifflin, 1942), p. 151; "The Use of Electrically Recorded Interviews in Improving Psychotherapeutic Techniques," *American Journal of Orthopsychiatry* 12 (1942): 429-434.

[21] Rogers, *Counseling and Psychotherapy*, pp. 25-28,195-196,439-440.

[22] Rogers, "Significant Aspects of Client-centered Therapy," *American Psychologist* 1 (1946): 415-22; "Psychotherapy," in W. Dennis (Ed.), *Current Trends in Psychotherapy* (Pittsburgh: University of Pittsburgh Press, 1947), pp. 109-137.

[23] Rogers, "A Teacher-Therapist Deals With a Handicapped Child," *Journal of Abnormal Social Psychology* 40 (1945): 119-142; *Client-Centered Therapy*, pp. 197-218; *On Becoming a Person*, p. 81; Evans, *Rogers*, p. 30.

[24] Rogers, "A Theory of Therapy," pp. 191, 248; "Dialogue Between Martin Buber and Carl Rogers," *Psychologia* 3 (1960): 208-221; *On Personal Power*, pp. 16-18; "Person-Centered," p. 128.

[25] R. J. DeCarvalho, *The Founders*, chap. 6.

[26] Rogers, *On Becoming a Person*, p. 200; "Autobiography," p. 378; "The Changing Theory of Client-centered Therapy," in A. Burton (Ed.), *Operational Theories of Personality* (New York: Brunner/Mazel, 1974), pp. 211-258. G. W. Allport, *Becoming* (New Haven: Yale University Press, 1955), p. 81; *Letters from Jenny* (New York: Harcourt, Brace & World, 1957), p. 11. R. R. May "The Existential Theory and Therapy," in J. H. Masserman (Ed.) *Current Psychiatric Therapies* (New York: Grune & Stratton, 1963), vol. 3, pp. 74-81; *Psychology and the Human Dilemma* (New York: Norton, 1967), p. 87; "Existentialism, Psychotherapy and the Problem of Death," in R. L. Shin (Ed.), *Restless Adventure* (New York: Scribner, 1968), p. 191. Evans, *Rogers*, p. 70; Maslow, *Towards a Psychology of Being* (New York: Nostrand, 1962), pp. 9-17.

[27] Rogers, "A Personal Formulation of Client-Centered Therapy," *Marriage & Family Living* 14 (1952): 341-61; "Persons or Science?" p. 199;

"Martin Buber and Carl Rogers," p. 208; *On Becoming a Person*, p. 273; Evans, *Rogers*, p. 69.

[28] Soren Kierkegaard, *Fear and Trembling and the Sickness Unto Death* (trans. by W. Lowrie from the Danish original, 1843) (Garden City: Doubleday, 1954), p. 29. Rogers, *Counseling and Psychotherapy*, pp. 208-210; "Therapy in Guidance Clinics," *Journal of Abnormal Social Psychology* 38 (1943): 284-89; "What it Means to Become a Person," in C. E. Moustakas (Ed.), *The Self* (New York: Harper, 1956), pp. 195-211; *On Becoming a Person*, pp. 166,172,199; "Foundations of the Person-Centered Approach," *Education* 100 (1979): 98-107.

[29] In 1957, Maurice Friedman, a Buber scholar, was instrumental in arranging a public dialogue between Rogers and Buber at the University of Michigan. This dialogue is particularly useful in delineating the points of agreement and disagreement between Buber and Rogers. See Rogers, "Martin Buber and Carl Rogers"; "A Basic Orientation for Counseling," *Pastoral Psychology* 1 (1950): 26-34; "A Personal Formulation," p. 342; "Persons or Science?" p. 290; "A Humanistic Conception of Man," in R. E. Farson (Ed.) *Science and Human Affairs* (Palo Alto: Science & Behavior Books, 1965), pp. 18-31; *A Way of Being*, p. 175; Evans, *Rogers*, pp. 25,69.

[30] Jean-Paul Sartre, *Being and Nothingness* (trans. H.E. Barnes from the French original, 1943) (New York: Washington Square Press, 1956), p. 725.

[31] Rogers, "Interview-b," pp. 87-90; "An Encounter with Carl Rogers," p. 45; "Foundations."

[32] Rogers, "A Theory of Therapy," p. 251; "Some Thoughts," p. 183; *Dialogue Between Paul Tillich and Carl Rogers* (San Diego: San Diego State College, 1966), p. 5; Evans, *Rogers*, p. 70; A. H. Maslow, *Farther Reaches of Human Nature* (New York: Viking, 1971), p. 186.

[33] Rogers, "Some Observations on the Organization of Personality," *American Psychologist* 2 (1947): 358-68; *Client-centered Therapy*, chap. 11; Rogers (Ed.), *Psychotherapy and Personality Change* (Chicago: University of Chicago Press, 1954), pp. 9,429-430; "Towards a Science," p. 77; "The Changing Theory," p. 255; Evans, *Rogers*, p. 9.

[34] R. J. DeCarvalho, *The Founders*, chap. 7.

[35] Rogers, *Client-Centered Therapy*, pp. 481,489; "Client-Centered

Therapy," p. 193; "Foundations," p. 100.

[36] Rogers, "Some Observations"; *Client-Centered Therapy*, pp. 481-533; "What it Means"; "The Process Equation of Psychotherapy," *American Journal of Psychotherapy* 15 (1961): 27-45; "The Changing Theory."

[37] Rogers, "Intellectualized Psychotherapy," *Contemporary Psychology* 1 (1956): 357-58; "Psychotherapy Today: Or, Where Do We Go From Here?" *American Journal of Psychotherapy* 17 (1963): 11; "The Process Equation."

[38] Rogers, "Some Observations," p. 366; *Client-Centered Therapy*, pp. 57, 481-533; "Autobiography," pp. 366,383; "The Changing Theory," p. 256; Evans, *Rogers*, p. 28.

[39] R. J. DeCarvalho, *The Founders*, chap. 8. The following citations refer to statements by Rogers on the crucial role of a concept of human nature in social thinking. Rogers, "Significant Aspects," p. 418; "Divergent Trends," p. 17; "A Basic Orientation," p. 26; "A Personal Formulation," p. 352; "A Note on the Nature of Man," *Pastoral Psychology* 11 (1957): 23-26.

[40] R. J. DeCarvalho, *The Founders*, chap. 8.

[41] Rogers' view of human nature permeates almost everything he wrote after *Counseling and Psychotherapy* (1942). The following references, however, are particularly relevant to this section, *On Becoming a Person*, pp. 31-38,107-124,183-196; "The Actualizing Tendency in Relation to "Motives" and to Consciousness," in M. R. Jones (Ed.), *Nebraska Symposium on Motivation* (Lincoln: University of Nebraska Press, 1963), pp. 1-24; "The Concept of the Fully Functioning Person," *Psychotherapy: Theory, Research and Practice* 1 (1963): 17-26; "Towards a Science of the Person"; "A Humanistic Conception"; "Person-Centered"; "Foundations"; "Reply to Rollo May's Letter to Carl Rogers," *Journal of Humanistic Psychology* 22 (1982): 85-89.

[42] Rogers, "Foundations," p. 101.

[43] Rogers, *Client-Centered Therapy*, p. 522; *On Becoming a Person*, p. 186; "Interview-b," pp. 87-89; "Foundations," p. 103.

[44] Rogers, *On Becoming a Person*, pp. 27,122; "What it Means," p. 206; *Martin Buber and Carl Rogers*, p. 171; "Fully Functioning Person", pp. 17-26.

[45] Rogers, *On Becoming a Person*, pp. 33-36,60; "The Necessary and

Sufficient Conditions of Therapeutic Personality Change," *Journal of Consulting Psychology* 21 (1957): 95-103; "Foundations," p. 98; "Person-Centered Approach," in R. Corsini (Ed.), *Encyclopedia of Psychology* (New York: Wiley, 1984), pp. 26-27.

Chapter 4

THE ETHICS OF THE GROWTH HYPOTHESIS[*]

The search for values has been moving forward in the social sciences. Not often, however, do social scientists venture into the philosopher's domain of ethics. Many even naively deny the significance of ethics in the social sciences; B. F. Skinner is a prime example. The founders of humanistic psychology, Gordon Allport, Abraham Maslow, Rollo May, Henry Murray, James Bugental, and Carl Rogers, were exceptions. Indeed, no other group of thinkers in the history and systems of psychology were as concerned with the problems of values as this group.[1]

Maslow and Rogers were certain that human beings need a value system, a system of understanding, or frame of orientation that gives life meaning and purpose. Unfortunately, they also pointed out, we live in an age where the ultimate disease is amorality, rootlessness, emptiness, hopelessness, lack of something in which to believe and to be devoted to. They blamed this modern uncertainty in value orientation on the anachronism between rigid ethical systems of the past and the relativistic world-view of

---

[*] Adapted from "The Ethics of the Growth Hypothesis of Abraham Maslow and Carl Rogers," *Journal of Ethical Studies*, 6(3), 1991, pp., 3-17, with the permission of the International Association of Ethicists, Inc.

science. Traditional ethics have failed, they explained, because their validation, sought in supernatural concepts, sacred books, or a ruling class, was *a
priori* authoritarian thinking. Science, on the other hand, since it has divorced
itself from ethical quests, has not offered any alternative. No longer unques-
tionably accepting the value systems of our upbringing, we find ourselves in
the dilemma of having to choose among various and, at times, contradictory
values. Not surprisingly, the modern person questions whether there are
universal or cross-cultural values.[2]

The solution to the ethical dilemmas of the modern age, suggested
Rogers and Maslow, was to find a "true" validating ethical system that is
independent of subjective values; or in Maslow's words, a system "based
squarely upon knowledge of the nature of man."[3] Like Maslow, Rogers also
complained that the study of ethics has always been in the domain of philosophy. He insisted that it was now the turn of the psychologists to initiate
scientific studies of values. It was in this context that Maslow and Rogers
persistently sought a naturalistic system of ethics. Their questions laid the
foundation for the emergence and establishment of a humanistic movement
in American psychology in the late 1950s and 1960s.[4]

Both Maslow and Rogers conceived an essential, intrinsic and un-
changeable biological reality in human nature that should be studied scientifically. Maslow was critical of psychological attempts to explain human nature
on the basis of the knowledge of sick individuals who sought the help of
psychologists. He selected for study those who, in his judgment, were the
"most fully human" and healthy individuals. He thought that their "humanness," capacities and values could represent the ultimate transcendental
values of the entire species.[5] Rogers, on the other hand, believed that the
contemporary problem and solution to the lack of values was microcosmical-
ly represented in his work on client-centered therapy. He studied people
who, in the process of psychotherapy grow towards psychological maturity
and health.[6] Both Rogers and Maslow concluded that there were universal

values that were an integral part of human nature; values which were experienced when the individual was in touch with his or her own organism. Organismic awareness, in their opinion, could help the individual to find within himself or herself a system of universal ethics that would answer the most perplexing value questions of our age. Such values were synonymous with psychological or physical health--concrete observable facts--and not mere subjective phenomena. They were as biologically based and descriptive as the concept of physical health was. Rogers and Maslow were convinced that such scientific study of human values would help formulate a naturalistic system of ethics. In Maslow's words,

> We can, in principle, have a descriptive, naturalistic science of values; that the age-old mutually exclusive contrast between "what is" and "what ought to be" is in part a false one; that we can study the highest values or goals of human beings as we study the values of ants or horses or oak trees, or, for that matter, Martians. We can discover (rather than create or invent) which values men trend toward, yearn for, struggle for, as they improve themselves, and which values they lose as they get sick.[7]

The Development of Maslow's Ethics

Maslow first wrote on ethics under the banner of cultural relativism in a 1937 essay on "Personality and Patterns of Culture." Although he acknowledged that values are relative to culture and that there are no universal norms of conduct, he recognized that there are biologically determined human universalities or a "basic temperamental make-up."[8] By the early 1940s, his studies in self-actualization convinced him that there are, indeed, underlying universal values that transcend culture. Most of these studies appeared in *Motivation and Personality* (1954), where he advanced a humanistic view of human nature and a naturalistic system of ethics. He thought that the values of the finest and most healthy individuals could serve as a model for the less fortunate.

In 1957, convinced that there was an urgent need for a science of ethics, Maslow organized and chaired a conference sponsored by the Research Society for Creative Altruism on "New Knowledge on Human Values." The papers presented at the conference were published two years later in a volume of the same title.[9]

In the 1960s, he thought that it was not enough just to improve persons; society could also be improved as a whole if the right values were implemented. Self-actualization could be fostered via social structures, if proper synergistic conditions were provided. In *Toward a Psychology of Being* (1962), he named this task "normative social psychology." In this context, his work, *Eupsychian Management* (1965), discussed the conditions, organization and kinds of work, management, and rewards that help people to grow healthier and to realize their full potential.[10]

In *The Psychology of Science* (1966), he expanded the critique of scientific method which was first advanced in *Motivation and Personality* (1954). He indicated that the inordinate stress on methods and techniques in science was largely motivated by the desire to avoid questions of value. He also argued that a value-free, or value-avoiding social science is unsuitable for the study of human nature. He advocated this standpoint as part of what he called a humanized philosophy, or normative biology.[11]

In *Religion, Values and Peak-Experiences* (1964), he argued that there is a higher and transcendental human nature. He stated that there is no longer a need for supernatural sanction of spiritual and mystical experiences and values; these have a naturalistic meaning and sanction.

A special section on values in *Farther Reaches of Human Nature* (1971), published posthumously, contained Maslow's final writings on ethics. He passed away in 1970 while working on a theory of evil.[12]

The Development of Rogers' Ethics

Rogers' first concise statement of client-centered therapy in *Counseling and Psychotherapy* (1942) was also his first venture into the philosopher's domain of ethics. In the context of the distinction between directive versus nondirective counseling, he argued that genuine insight into one's condition leads to more positive choices, satisfaction, and personal growth.[13]

Throughout the 1940s he perfected this view while writing on the potential capacity of the human organism for self-understanding, self-direction, and growth. In these writings, a view of human nature emerges. Rogers argued that a person has a latent capacity for change and growth, but only the self can discover and free that potential. The task of psychotherapy was merely to make an alliance with these forces and facilitate their release.[14]

In *The Client-Centered Therapy* (1951), the concept of "organismic valuing process" is at the center of client-centered therapy. He clarified the significance for psychological health of being aware of one's continuing organismic valuing process.[15]

In *On Becoming a Person* (1961) he explicitly addressed the problem of ethics. Describing his views on personal goals from the standpoint of a therapist, he answered the following questions: "What is my goal in life," "What am I striving for," and "What is my purpose?" He synthesized his thoughts on values and ventured into the problem of evil as he discussed the implications for society, politics, and international relations.[16]

He also described the self-actualized healthy person. Borrowing from Kierkegaard the idea that the goal of life is "to be that self which one truly is," he thereby placed the existential concept of authenticity at the forefront of his views on ethics.[17]

Rogers summarized his thoughts on ethics in a paper entitled "Toward A Modern Approach To Values," a paper that defined his understanding of values in the context of client-centered therapy and his view of human nature. It was perhaps his most definitive statement on the subject.[18]

The Growth Hypothesis and View of Human Nature

Maslow and Rogers thought that it was impossible for a psychologist to be objective and not to have a view of human nature. A well-articulated view of human nature was, in their understanding, the most important value in science, for psychology in particular. Any psychological discipline deserving the name entails a view of human nature, they argued. Every one, including the most experimentally oriented psychologist, has an understanding of people, whether consciously stated or not. "The issue," wrote Maslow, "is thus not over whether or not to have a philosophy of psychology, but whether to have one that is conscious or unconscious."[19] The unconscious understandings or theories of human nature are particularly dangerous since they guide the collection of data and research more profoundly than laboriously acquired empirical knowledge. Rogers and Maslow argued, in other words, that there are prior personal, subjective views of human nature necessary in determining a purpose or value in scientific work. It is important that these values be stated and clarified since they cannot be tested, evaluated or denied by scientific means. In their own cases, they, indeed, dedicated much effort to the delineation of a view of human nature, represented in their interpretation of the growth hypothesis theory developed by Kurt Goldstein.[20]

Maslow argued that people have basic needs, emotions and capacities that are neutral, pre-moral, positive, and good. If these basic needs guide our lives, we grow healthier and happier; but if we deny or suppress them, sickness is virtually a certainty. In this view, there are higher and lower needs arranged in levels of potency in which the fulfillment of less potent needs relies upon the gratification of the more potent ones. The higher aspects of human nature, in other words, rest upon the fulfillment of the lower nature.[21]

Physiological needs related to basic survival, such as food, shelter, safety, and security, belong to the lower aspects of human nature and dominate the organism at the elementary level. When satisfied, however, the next higher need emerges and organizes the personality differently. Belonging, affection, love, respect, and self-esteem belong to the next level; self-actualization to another; and spiritual and transcendental needs constitute the last category. A healthy person is, according to Maslow, one who develops and actualizes his or her full potentialities and capacities by gratifying the ascending hierarchy of needs. Maslow called such persons "self-actualizers" because they sought to fulfill their inner potential. However, when a persistent, active, basic need is not satisfied, the person is not free to grow and fulfill the higher need, and is said to be ill.

> Self-actualization is intrinsic growth of what is already in the organism, or more accurately of what is the organism itself. Just as our tree needs food, sun, water from the environment, so does the person need safety, love, and status from the social environment. But as in the first case, so also in the second, this is just where real development, i.e., of individuality, begins. All trees need sunlight and all human beings need love, and yet, once satiated with these elementary necessities, each tree and each human being proceeds to develop in his own style, uniquely, using these universal necessities to his own private purposes.[22]

All needs, including the higher needs, are as "instinctoid" or physiological as, for example, the need for vitamins. Deprivation of safety, love, truth, joy and justice can generate a pathological state similar to that caused, for example, by the deprivation of vitamin C.[23]

Rogers' version of the growth hypothesis shares much in common with Maslow's self-actualization. Rogers thought that infants have a clear set of values. Infants choose experiences that induce growth, maintain and actualize their organismic potential, and reject what is contrary to their well-being.

Since the values that guide their actualization lie strictly within their organism, they are thus naturalistic and objective. But, Rogers argued, as infants grow, their efficient valuing process is lost, and slowly transformed into rigid, artificial, and organismically inefficient value systems. Their naive conception that what feels good is good becomes distorted by the assimilation of the evaluation of adults who, in exchange for love, make them feel sorry, fearful, and guilty about their values. In this process, they lose the wisdom of organismic awareness and incorporate the values set by the immediate human environment. The values carried along with the love, esteem, and approval from adults force them to distrust the experience of their own organism as a guiding value system. In other words, they relinquish their trust of organismic wisdom.[24]

When the discrepancy between organismic and assimilated artificial values is acute, the individual experiences questions of meaning which are cyclically originated by, or culminate, in personal crisis. This estrangement of people from themselves, according to Rogers, explains modern stress, insecurity, the lack of and the search for values. The goal of psychotherapy, he argued, is to reverse that process. By confronting the individual with the lack of contact with his or her own organism, psychotherapy puts the person back in touch with their organismic valuing process. In Rogers's words,

> I believe that when the human being is inwardly free to choose whatever he deeply values, he tends to value those objects, and goals which make for his own survival, growth, and development, and for the survival and development of others. I hypothesize that it is *characteristic* of the human organism to prefer such actualizing and socialized goals when he is exposed to a growth promoting climate.[25]

The belief that people have the capacity for self-understanding and reorganization if they are only provided the necessary and sufficient conditions for personality change, was the foundation of Rogers' client-centered therapy. Given an appropriate growth-inducing environment in which one is unconditionally accepted, one learns the causes of behavior and new ways of perceiving and reacting to these causes. Once the denied attitudes and behavior become conscious and accepted, the self assimilates them and reorganizes itself, consequently altering the entire personality structure and behavior. In other words, when one explores and accepts the inner self, one learns to be in touch with and release the organismic wisdom. If given freedom to become what one truly is, one's true identity is naturally actualized, which Rogers argued could only be positive in terms of enhancing the individual's nature and existence.[26]

The goal of client-centered therapy was to set the person free from internal and external barriers so that the basic nucleus of his or her nature would be released. In the early stages of therapy, people live largely by values introjected from others. As therapy progresses, however, they realize that they are living according to the expectations of others. When this acknowledgement becomes unbearable, their valuing process changes. The judgment and expectation of others concerning their thinking and feeling is slowly replaced by their own experience, values, and standards. In this understanding of client-centered therapy, Rogers implied that the basic nature of the person when functioning freely is constructive and trustworthy. Each one of us has capacity for self-understanding and for initiating change in the direction of psychological growth and maturity, provided only that we are genuinely free and treated with worth and significance. In this sense, he argued, the therapist merely makes an alliance with the individual's organismic forces pressing for growth and self-actualization.[27]

Authenticity and Psychotherapy

Rogers and Maslow's version of the growth hypothesis also referred to the ability of self-actualizers to transcend the environment. In this context, they criticized the identification of psychological health with the concept of adjustment. They thought that it was misleading to define a healthy person in environment-centered terms concerned with adjustment to reality, society or job: they argued that mental health should rather be defined in terms of the individual's autonomy and transcendence of the environment. It should be defined in terms of the ability to rely on or function within, yet transcend the social norms--the ability to stand against, fight, neglect, or change environmental conditions. The healthy, fully-grown person is not a willy-nilly product of public opinions. In this sense healthy people are, according to Maslow and Rogers, said to be authentic, original, and creative; but not necessarily well-adjusted.[28]

Not surprisingly, authenticity, rather than adjustment was, for Rogers and Maslow, also the goal of psychotherapy. Psychotherapy, they argued, should help the less fortunate to reach the level of authenticity, and the individuation found among self-actualizers. It meant, in Maslow's understanding, not to create, but to reveal or expose the biological core--the inborn preferences, talents, and yearnings of the individual; and to facilitate integration with these talents and yearnings.

The qualities of the biological core are not *a priori* "oughts" or "moral imperatives" in the old philosophical sense; but, rather, are intrinsic to the human nature of the individual. Denial and even absence of awareness of such a core lead to psychological illness, frustration, and disintegration. The task of psychotherapy was, thus, to train the person in authenticity; or, to help the individual gain identity through the discovery of the innate values that are part of his or her nature, but unknown to him or her. Psychotherapy was, in other words, the search for, and integration of one's own biologically intrinsic and authentic values. One's life problems, vocation, and decision making could be much easier if people knew what is easier for them to do--what fits or suits them better from the perspective of their organism.

Psychotherapy was, in this sense, a process of recovery of "specieshood" or of "healthy animality," of self-discovery, and of integration leading toward greater authenticity of being and spontaneous expressiveness.[29]

The Values of Self-Actualizers

Rogers' naturalistic understanding of values permeates his depiction of "fully functioning," healthy people. He described these persons as people who avoid presenting facades and do not pretend to be what they are not. They move away from what people think they ought to be, and do not fulfill expectations to please others. They deeply feel the immediacy of their experience, endeavoring to clarify its complexity. They are open to experience, open to see things in their inner and outer world as they are. Like infants, they explore and trust the wisdom of their organisms. Their centers of evaluation are within themselves--in their organismic awareness. They trust their feelings and intuitions more than they trust their minds and social norms. They are proud and confident of their choices. They are self-directed, autonomous, and responsible for their lives. They choose what is meaningful for them. When, however, the chosen course of action turns out to be wrong or deceptive; they readjust, revise, and accommodate to the new circumstances while continuously correcting their valuing process to obtain the maximum actualization of their potential. The criteria used in their valuing process change from situation to situation, and are congruent with the satisfaction to be obtained. They have no fixed or rigid goals, and are not always consistent. They are open, fluid, flexible, and always actualizing different facets of their being. Their behavior is unpredictable, and creative. They are, in other words, never the same, and always in a process of becoming.[30]

Maslow's description of self-actualizers is pretty similar to Rogers' "fully functioning person." Maslow described these people as integrated and having a strong sense of identity and individuality. They are autonomous, whole, and creative. They are "alive" and unique, rather than "dead" and stereotyped. They have a democratic character structure, and they are devoted to a mission or cause which they deeply believe in. They feel a vocation to final values or principles that, though they cannot be rationally validated, are felt to be good, and worth pursuing. They are confident about what they think is right and wrong, and make ethical judgments and decisions quicker than average people. They choose truth, good, beauty, joy, and fairness rather than evil, ugliness, sorrow, and prejudice. Though they have a firm and real sense of identity and an integrated self, when necessary, they also transcend that self. They are open to experience, have a clearer and more accurate perception of reality, and are, thus, more objective and detached. They have discovered their natural bent or "biological destiny," and exploit their unique capacities and talents in a naive, almost child-like manner.[31]

Maslow and Rogers agreed that a significant facet of self-actualizing people is their spontaneous expressiveness or authenticity of being. Both explained that such people consider the behavior and being they emit from within as good, trustworthy and ethical. They are alive and fully functioning and true to their inner self; in other words, they are authentic to their nature. The authenticity, values, and behavior of these people are held to be descriptive qualities of psychological health. And, since they are better perceivers and choosers, they naturally choose, in biological terms, what is growth inducing and good for them. Since they are human beings, it follows that their values could be the eternal verities or, according to Maslow, the Being-values of all people (e.g., what is good species-wide). If the values of self-actualizers induce growth and health in the best members of the species, then, perhaps, such values are ideals to be prescribed to the less fortunate. Knowledge of their ethics could serve as a beacon, or model for the conduct, control, and improvement of our lives.[32]

Free Will, Determinism and Evil

In this context, Rogers and Maslow had a new perspective on the age-old philosophical problem of freedom versus determinism. "Fully functioning" or "self-actualizing" people, they argued, are free people. In the process of choosing courses of action that are most satisfying they exercise free will. Neurotics, on the other hand, are defensively organized. They follow settled rigid patterns of feelings and behavior over which they have little or no control, patterns that are determined. Free will is, in this sense, a by-product of psychological health, of organismic awareness, and choice. Conversely, absence of free will also explained the existence of evil. They similarly argued that there is no such thing as an innate actualizing tendency toward destructiveness, or the fulfilling of an evil nature.[33]   *it's more subtle them that —*

In Rogers' understanding, evil is a product of social conditioning and voluntary choice. He pointed out that when people first begin psychotherapy, they feel that if they become what they truly are, their behavior will be bad, evil, uncontrollable, and destructive: that they will release the beast within themselves. But, in the course of psychotherapy, as they experience and express hostile feelings, they realize that they are not evil. As a matter of fact, the more one permits evil feelings to surface the less potent and burdensome they become. The more one becomes what one truly is, the less evil one finds within and the more one becomes sensitive, responsive, and creative. "A person with relatively good understanding of himself and his situation," wrote Rogers, "was far less likely to become delinquent."[34] When in the process of psychotherapy delinquents and criminals become fully functioning and actu- alizing people, they do not become better criminals, but rather choose more constructive and positive behavior.[35]

Maslow explored the problem of evil only toward the end of his life. Like Rogers, Maslow also thought that the major sources of evil (such as cruelty, destructiveness, sadism, malice, etc.) were not intrinsic to human nature, but violent reactions against frustration of the most basic and prepotent of our hierarchical needs. This frustration results from the lack of authenticity or integration with one's own nature. In this sense, ignorance of one's true nature was the major source of evil behavior. Evil choices result in evil behavior. Truth and virtue, like ignorance and evil, are synonymous concepts. He thus wrote that he agreed with the Socratic saying "no man with full knowledge could ever do evil." Rogers would have concurred.[36]

Conclusion

The growth hypothesis of Kurt Goldstein was a source of inspiration for Carl Rogers and Abraham Maslow, whose studies on self-actualization served as a foundation for the establishment of the humanistic movement in American psychology. Their versions of the growth hypothesis also dictated their understanding of human nature and naturalistic ethics. Maslow studied psychologically healthy people and the hierarchy of biological needs. Rogers studied the process of growth experienced by patients in client-centered psychotherapy.

Their views on ethics stemmed from a basic trust of the worthiness of human nature. They argued that when people are authentic, experience their inner worlds, and function free from internal and external barriers; they value and choose (from an organismic point of view) what is good for them. Although the self-selected process and direction of becoming are subjective, and thus relative from individual to individual; the choices of self-actualizing or fully functioning people, they argued, embody the species-wide intrinsic values of human nature conducive to psychological health. These choices and values, therefore, ought to be the guiding principles of human conduct for the less fortunate. Their choices and values ought to be the basis for a universal and naturalistic system of ethics. Such system was not, they argued, *a priori*. Since they were testable, anyone scientifically studying the same people will arrive at similar conclusions. Kierkegaard's phrase, "To be that self which one truly is," is synonymous with the seeking of authenticity, the highest value in Rogers and Maslow's naturalistic system of ethics. In Maslow's words authenticity was "truthfulness to one's own nature."

ENDNOTES

[1] R. J. DeCarvalho, *The Founders of Humanistic Psychology* (New York: Praeger, 1991); "A History of the 'Third Force' in Psychology," *Journal of Humanistic Psychology* 30 (1990): 22-44; "The Growth Hypothesis and Self-Actualization: An Existential Alternative," *The Humanistic Psychologist* 18 (1990): 252-258.

[2] Rogers, "The Developing Values of the Growing Person," *The Psychiatric Institute Bulletin* (University of Wisconsin) 1 (1961): 1-15; "Toward a Modern Approach to Values: The Valuing Process in the Mature Person," *Journal of Abnormal Social Psychology* 68 (1964): 160-167; R. I. Evans, *Carl Rogers: The Man and His Ideas* (New York: Dutton, 1975), p. 101.

[3] Maslow, *New Knowledge in Human Values* (New York: Harper, 1959), p. viii.

[4] Maslow, *Religion, Values and Peak-Experiences* (Columbus: Ohio State University Press, 1964), pp. 3,38,82; *Farther Reaches of Human Nature* (New York: Viking, 1971), p. 377. Rogers, *To Be That Self Which One Truly Is: A Therapist's View of Personal Goals* (Transcript of a Talk at the College of Wooster, Ohio on March 14, 1957); "The Developing Values"; "The Formative Tendency," *Journal of Humanistic Psychology* 18 (1978): 23-26.

[5] Maslow, *New Knowledge*, pp. 127,245; "Some Frontier Problems in Mental Health," in A. Combs (Ed.), *Personality Theory and Counseling Practice* (Miami: University of Florida Press, 1961), pp. 1-13; *Toward a Psychology of Being* (New York: Nostrand, 1962), pp. 3-8,74,167,205; *Religion, Values and Peak-Experience*, pp. 82,97-102; *Farther Reaches*, pp. 9-10,135-151.

[6] Rogers, "A Therapist View of the Good Life," *The Humanist* 17 (1957): 291-300; "Toward a Modern Approach"; "The Formative Tendency."

[7] Maslow, *Psychology of Being*, p. 167. See also pp. 3-8,74,205; and, *New Knowledge*, pp. 127,245; "Some Frontier Problems," p. 8; *Religion, Values and Peak-Experiences*, pp. 82,97-102; *Farther Reaches*, pp. 9,135-151.

[8] Maslow, "Personality and Patterns of Culture," in R. Stagner (Ed.), *Psychology of Personality* (New York: McGraw-Hill, 1937), p. 428.

[9] Maslow, *New Knowledge*.

[10] Maslow, "Eupsychia-The Good Society," *Journal of Humanistic Psychology* 1 (1961): 1-11; *Psychology of Being*, pp. 211,220-222; *Religion, Values and Peak-Experiences*, p. 102; *Eupsychian Management: A Journal* (Homewood: Irwin-Dorsey, 1965), p. 3; *Farther Reaches*, pp. 212-225.

[11] Maslow, *Motivation and Personality* (New York: Harper, 1954), p. 20; *Religion, Values and Peak-Experiences*, pp. 11-13; *The Psychology of Science: A Reconnaissance* (New York: Harper and Row, 1966), chap. 12, pp. 119-127; *Motivation and Personality* (New York: Harper and Row, rev. ed., 1970), p. xxiii; *Farther Reaches*, pp. 3-24,43,173.

[12] E. Hoffman, *The Right to be Human: A Biography of Abraham Maslow* (Los Angeles: Jeremy P. Tarcher, 1988), p. 332.

[13] Rogers, *Counseling and Psychotherapy* (Boston: Houghton Mifflin, 1942), pp. 39-43,126-128,208.

[14] Rogers, "Therapy in Guidance Clinics," *Journal of Abnormal and Social Psychology* 38 (1943): 284-289; "Psychotherapy," in W. Dennis (Ed.), *Current Trends in Psychotherapy* (Pittsburgh: University of Pittsburgh Press, 1947), pp. 109-137; "The Role of Self-Understanding in the Prediction of Behavior," *Journal of Consulting Psychology* 12 (1948): 174-186; "A Basic Orientation for Counseling," *Pastoral Psychology* 1 (1950): 26-34; "What Is to be Our Basic Professional Relationship?" *Annals of Allergy* 8 (1950): 234-239.

[15] Rogers, *Client-Centered Therapy: Its Current Practice, Implications, and Theory* (Boston: Houghton Mifflin, 1951), pp. 71, 139, 522.

[16] Rogers, *To Be That Self*; "Dialogue Between Martin Buber and Carl Rogers," *Psychologia* 3 (1960): 208-221.

[17] Rogers, "A Therapist View."

[18] Rogers, "The Developing Values"; "Toward a Modern Approach."

[19] Maslow, "A Philosophy of Psychology," in F. T. Severin (Ed.), *Humanistic Viewpoints in Psychology* (New York: McGraw-Hill, 1956), p. 23.

[20] Rogers, "A Personal View of Some Issues Facing Psychologists," *American Psychologist* 10 (1955): 247-249; *On Becoming a Person* (Boston: Houghton Mifflin, 1961), p. 391; C. R. Rogers & B. F. Skinner, "Some Issues Concerning the Control of Human Behavior," In R. I. Evans, *Carl Rogers: The Man and His Ideas* (New York: Dutton, 1975), pp. xiiv-lxxxviii. Maslow, *Motivation and Personality*, pp. 6-12; "A Philosophy of Psychology," pp. 17-33; *Psychology of Being*, chap. 1, pp. 189-214; W. B. Frick, *Humanistic Psychology: Interviews with Maslow, Murphy and Rogers* (Columbus: Merrill, 1971), pp. 22-32.

[21] Maslow, *Motivation and Personality*, pp. 107-122,146-154,183,379; "Deficiency Motivation and Growth Motivation," in M. R. Jones (Ed.), *Nebraska Symposium in Motivation* (Lincoln: University of Nebraska Press, 1955), pp. 1-30; *Psychology of Science*, pp. 119-127.

[22] Maslow, *Motivation and Personality*, p. 183.

[23] Maslow, *Motivation and Personality*, pp. 1-30,179; "Some Frontier Problem"; *Psychology of Being*, p. 206; Frick, *Humanistic Psychology*, p. 32; T. B. Roberts, "Maslow's Motivation Needs Hierarchy: A Bibliography," *Research in Education* (ED-069-591, 1971).

[24] Rogers, *Client-Centered Therapy*, p. 522; "The Developing Values."

[25] Rogers, "Toward a Modern Approach," p. 166; cf., *Client-Centered Therapy*, pp. 139,141.

[26] Rogers, "Therapy in Guidance Clinics," p. 285; "The Role of Self-understanding"; "Basic Professional Relationship," p. 236; *Client-Centered Therapy*, p. 71; *On Becoming a Person*, p. 87.

[27] Rogers, "Psychotherapy," p. 113; "A Basic Orientation," *Client-Centered Therapy*, pp. 75,149,157, 530; "Learning to be Free," in S. M. Farber & R. H. Wilson (Eds.), *Conflict and Creativity: Control of the Mind* (New York: McGraw-Hill, 1963), part 2, pp. 268-288; *Becoming Partners: Marriage and its Alternatives* (New York: Delacorte, 1972), p. 208.

[28] Maslow, *Motivation and Personality*, pp. 291-304,379-390; *New Knowledge*, p. 131; *Psychology of Being*, p. 179; *Farther Reaches*, pp. 51-53,185-187. Rogers, *On Becoming a Person*, pp. 31,107; "Toward a Modern Approach"; "The Formative Tendency."

[29] Maslow, *Motivation and Personality*, pp. 213,224-228,389; "Eupsychia," p. 5; *Psychology of Being*, pp. 176-178; *Farther Reaches*, p. 186. Rogers, *On Becoming a Person*; "Toward a Modern Approach"; "The Formative Tendency."

[30] Rogers, "What it Means to Become a Person," in C. E. Moustakas (Ed.), *The Self* (New York: Harper, 1956), pp. 195-211; "A Therapist View"; *On Becoming a Person*, pp. 163-182,183-198; "Learning to be Free"; "Toward a Modern Approach," p. 166; *Becoming Partners*, p. 208.

[31] Maslow, *Religion, Values and Peak-Experiences*, pp. 91-96; "The Farther Reaches of Human Nature," *Journal of Transpersonal Psychology* 1 (1968): 1-9; *Goals of Humanistic Education* (Big Sur: Esalen Papers, 1968), pp. 18-24; *Farther Reaches*, pp. 43, 122-125,133-135,192-195,299-340; Frick, *Humanistic Psychology*, p. 32.

[32] Maslow, *Motivation and Personality*, pp. 199-234,230-232; *New Knowledge*, pp. 119-136; *Psychology of Being*, pp. 81-84; *Eupsychian Management*, pp. 119-121.

[33] Rogers, "A Therapist View," p. 192; M. Friedman, "Comment on the Rogers-May Discussion of Evil," *Journal of Humanistic Psychology* 22 (1982): 93-96.

[34] Frick, *Humanistic Psychology*, p. 89.

[35] Rogers, "The Role of Self-Understanding"; *On Becoming a Person*, pp. 177, 344; Frick, *Humanistic Psychology*, p. 89; R. Bayne, "An Encounter with Carl Rogers and R. D. Laing," *Bulletin of the British Psychological Society* 32 (1979): 99-100.

[36] Maslow, "Some Frontier Problems," p. 8; *Psychology of Being*, p. 195; "Conversation with Abraham H. Maslow," *Psychology Today* 2 (1968): 36; *Farther Reaches*, p. 124. Rogers, *On Becoming a Person*, p. 163.

Chapter 5

THE HUMANISTIC PARADIGM IN EDUCATION[*]

Humanistic psychology was founded as an alternative to the dominant behavioristic and psychoanalytical orientation in psychology. As the humanistic orientation in psychology developed into a distinct discipline, it began to extend its influence into other areas. Education, in particular, which had fallen under the influence of behaviorism, was to feel the impact of the humanistic view point.

As Rogers, who was known for his student-centered approach, and Maslow, who was known for his views on intrinsic learning, became aware of the implications of humanistic psychology on educational theory and practice, they sought to create a humanistic paradigm in that field. A study of this humanistic paradigm in education remains as meaningful today as it was two decades ago.

Maslow and Rogers were certain that humans need a value system, a system of understanding, or frame of orientation that gives life meaning and reason. But unfortunately, they argued, we live in an age in which the ulti-

---

[*] Adapted with permission from R. J. DeCarvalho, "The Humanistic Paradigm in Education," *The Humanistic Psychologist* 19 (1991).

mate disease is amorality, rootlessness, emptiness, hopelessness, lack of belief and devotion. They blamed this modern uncertainty in value orientation on the anachronism between rigid ethical systems of the past and the ethical relativism of science. No longer unquestioningly accepting the value systems of our upbringing, we as a society find ourselves in the dilemma of having to choose among various and, at times, even contradictory values. This confusion in value orientation is obviously reflected in the educational system.[1]

The crisis in American education, they argued, results from the lack of values concerning the purpose and goal, in other words, the ultimate value, of the acquisition of knowledge. In order to evade issues of values in the curriculum, educators turned to what they mistakenly believed was a value-free mechanistic and technological education. Both Rogers and Maslow thus bitterly complained about the overly technological and behavioristic emphasis in American education--as if education was merely technological training for the acquisition of skills that were value-free or amoral. Instead of facilitating the personal growth of the whole child, educators rather trained children in skills designed to make them efficient in and adjusted to a technological society which, although unrecognized, is in itself also a reflection of values.[2]

Rogers and Maslow's answer to this problem is derived from their growth hypothesis' view of human nature. They thought that the ultimate goal of education was to facilitate the students' self-actualization of their potential; to help them become the best human beings that they are capable of becoming. Or as Rogers described it, "to be that self which one truly is."[3]

The Development of Maslow's Views on Education

Maslow's college education was rooted in the best behavioristic tradition. His MA thesis at the University of Wisconsin-Madison, an experimental study of the effect of varying simple external conditions on learning, was also his first education-related research project. Soon after graduation, however, he departed from the behavioristic approach. Maslow's studies of dominance among female college students led him to develop the needs hierarchy theory of human motivation that made him famous. These studies, gathered in part in *Motivation and Personality* (1954), advanced a humanistic view of human nature that became an important pillar of the humanistic movement in American psychology. His distinction in this work between expressive and coping behavior, and his views on self-actualization became the bases of his later discussion of intrinsic and expressive learning in education. For Maslow, coping behavior was a response to operant conditioning dealing with matters of basic survival, while expressive behavior was seen as a spontaneous expression of a person's basic character leading to the actualization of inner potential.[4]

In the 1960s Maslow's writings emphasized creativity and its significance in teaching. He argued that teaching creativity through art should become the paradigm for all other fields of education. Maslow's *Farther Reaches of Human Nature* (1971), published posthumously, was a compilation of much of his work on this theme. This book also included a section on education which contained various essays written in the late 1960s on the values, goals, and implications of humanistic education. Maslow drew on the early distinction between expressive and coping behavior, defining intrinsic learning as the humanistic paradigm in education. He argued that educators should, in a sense, form an alliance with the organismic forces conducive to the fulfillment of the students potential and growth toward self-actualization. Concurrently Maslow criticized extrinsic learning and coping behavior, blaming these core concepts of the behavioristic paradigm for the failures of the American educational system.

The Development of Rogers' Views on Education

By 1952, Rogers was pessimistic about his teaching and education in general. Losing interest in education, he believed that it was impossible to really teach anything to anyone. Seven years later, in 1959, he was more optimistic; he published an article entitled "The Significant Learning: In Psychotherapy and in Education," which applied the learning process in psychotherapy to education. During the next eight years, he expanded and refined the ideas advanced in this article. In essence, Rogers believed that educators were not really teachers, but facilitators.[5]

At the age of 62, disappointed with the educational system at the University of Wisconsin-Madison, Rogers joined the Western Behavioral Sciences Institute in La Jolla, California, and for three years (1965-1968) he tried out his education program in practice. He proposed a plan adaptable to any educational system interested in innovative change. Several school systems answered Rogers' call and aided by grants from different sources, Rogers chose the Immaculate Heart College system, which comprised several high schools and elementary schools in the Los Angeles area. Three years later, Rogers proudly claimed to have initiated self-directed change in a large educational system; the college had been successfully working under Rogers' plan independent of personal contact with Rogers or his group for two years.[6]

Believing his ideas represented a revolution in education, Rogers began to collect reports from educators who were attempting to put his ideas into practice. In 1969, he compiled some of these reports in *Freedom to Learn-A View of What Education Might Become* (1969), a book that became the bible of humanistic education. Selling 40,000 copies in the first year of publication, the book showed how educators could be personal, innovative, and facilitative of learning even within an antiquated system. With the success of *Freedom to Learn*, Rogers continued to write for teachers' periodicals on personal growth, teaching, and the future of education.[7]

Critique of Behaviorism

Rogers and Maslow participated in a persistent and, at times, even bitter debate with the behaviorists on the nature and scope of the social sciences. They also criticized behaviorism in education. Behaviorists, such as Skinner, thought that advances in the study and control of behavior would make education a new "branch of technological science." In "The Science of Learning and the Art of Teaching," Skinner stated that certain techniques of reinforcement shape the behavior of an organism at the will of the experimenter. The precision of control is proportional to the precision of the manipulation of complex techniques of reinforcement, which consist of carefully designed multiple schedules of reinforcement followed by changing contingencies. Education for democracy and for life were trivial pursuits that soon would be replaced by the principles of scientific technological education. Moreover, the advances in scientific technological education, Skinner argued, made human teachers outdated. He thus described in some detail the designing and marketing of teaching machines. In other words, Skinner was arguing for the dehumanization of education. Indeed, his social utopia, *Walden Two* (1948), pictured a civilization whose members had been brought up by a complex control of machinery and a cast of expert social technicians.[8]

Rogers and Maslow were more than critical of Skinner's behavioristic educational philosophy; they blamed such a philosophy for the failure of American education. They thought that behaviorism lacked systematic and valid concepts of human behavior and learning, aiming to cultivate and enforce desired behavior as if people were pigeons or laboratory rats. The consequence was that education became a mere impinging of a chosen technological, mechanistic, and valueless curriculum so that the individual might not follow his or her own mistaken way.[9]

Maslow and Rogers thought that it was impossible for an educator to be objective and not to have a view of human nature. A well-articulated view of human nature was, in their understanding, the most important value necessary in education. Every educator has, whether consciously stated or not, an understanding of people. The issue, they thought, is not whether or not to have a philosophy of education, but whether to have one that is conscious or unconscious. Both argued, in other words, that educators bring into their world already existing subjective views of human nature and the purpose or value of education. It is important that these values be stated and clarified since they cannot be tested, evaluated, or denied by scientific means. In their case, they, indeed, dedicated much effort to the delineation of a view of human nature.[10] The cornerstone of Maslow and Rogers' views on human nature was the growth hypothesis, from which their naturalistic system of ethics and humanistic paradigm in education were derived. Maslow explained that an "instinctoid" inner core of human nature contains potentialities pressing for actualization. Similarly, Rogers stated that the human organism has a directional and actualizing tendency toward the fulfillment of inner potential. Both were inspired by Kurt Goldstein.

Rogers and Maslow counterposed the understanding of human nature contained in the growth hypothesis to the positivistic philosophy of behaviorism, and believed that true learning is possible only when it is intrinsic, experiential, significant or meaningful. When one learns something, one is experiencing a process of discovery that is real and an integral part of the character structure. A good illustration is a child who, in his free will, goes to the library in order to satisfy his curiosity about earthworms or sex. The essence of this type of learning is its personal intrinsic meaning. When one has a need to learn and is free to choose what to learn, the knowledge acquired becomes meaningful and a source of satisfaction. Self-initiated knowledge has the quality of personal involvement. Thus the purpose of education, according to Rogers and Maslow, was not external conditioning and enforcement of learning habits, as Skinner had argued, but rather to stimulate curiosity, the inner need to discover and explore, to facilitate personal involvement and, of course, to supply the necessary instructional resources.[11]

The most important value and goal of education according to Maslow and Rogers' humanistic paradigm was to facilitate the students' discovery and actualization of their nature and vocation. In other words, to help them discover what they are good at and what they enjoy doing. The learning that resulted from this need has subjective meaning and results in expressive and creative behavior that is personally satisfying. In this sense, the goal of education was to make an alliance with the student's natural wonder and to facilitate the process of learning. This type of learning changes a person from within, promoting psychological health and growth toward the actualization of their human potential.[12]

Intrinsic learning and self-discovery, they argued, are related concepts in the sense that the latter enables students to look inward and from inner knowledge derive their own subjective values. Education becomes a vital means of discovery of identity, training in authenticity and self-fulfillment. A good example is the discovery of one's professional vocation. When found, the process to acquire the knowledge requisite to that vocation has personal meaning that becomes an integral part of personality independent of reinforcing stimulus. Maslow and Rogers concluded that it is important for the educational system to induce students to explore their organismic potential as a vital part of training in their self-chosen professional or scholarly field. An educational system based on these principles, they argued, will turn out much more creative people.[13]

Maslow's Intrinsic Learning

Maslow thought that contemporary American education failed because it focused on extrinsic and coping behavior rather than on expressive behavior and intrinsic learning. His later distinction between extrinsic and intrinsic learning followed his understanding of expressive and coping behavior first argued within terms of the need-hierarchy theory of motivation. Maslow blamed behaviorists for focusing exclusively on coping behavior, which, he argued, was the least significant part of personality. Coping behavior is functional, instrumental, adaptive, and the product of an interaction of the character-structure with the world. Coping behavior is learned or acquired in order to deal with specific environmental situations, and dies out if not rewarded or continuously bombarded with stimulus. Since the extrinsic knowledge ensuing from coping behavior is forcefully implanted by operant conditioning or indoctrination, it is never an integral part of personality and thus not perceived as meaningful. The conditioning must be reinforced continuously, otherwise the learning disappears. This type of learning focuses on techniques that are interchangeable and result in automatic habits such as driving or swimming. It is useful learning, but meaningless as far as growth and actualization of the inner character structure. Problem solving, for example, ensues from a memorized response rather than from understanding the problem and reacting creatively. In fact, understanding is inimical to behavioral operant conditioning. When conditioning ceases or people understand that they are victims of conditioning, they rebel and dispose of the enforced learning. Earning a degree, reward for scholarly achievement, and other similar practices are by-products of extrinsic education.[14]

Extrinsic learning and coping behavior, Maslow argued, were the bases for the failure of contemporary American education. Students not only drop out of school because they find little personal meaning in the process of learning, but they also rebel against the system in order to assert their identity. The solution, he suggested, was to shift the educational system to the paradigm of intrinsic learning and expressive behavior. Expressive behavior, such as artistic creation, play, wonder, and love, is a reflection of personality. Since it is non-functional and persists without reward, it is an epiphenomenon of inner character-structure. Expressive behavior resulting from intrinsic learning has meaningful personal value and remains an integral part of the self even when external stimuli ceases.[15]

In regard to ability to predict behavior, Maslow compared external scientific control of the behavioristic type with the internal self-knowledge posited by humanistic psychology. He argued that people resent and rebel against external scientific control, but they accept the increase of self-knowledge that allows them to control their own behavior. Self-knowledge of the humanistic type has thus much more personal meaning and predictive power.[16]

A related and significant goal of education, according to Maslow, was to teach students skills--such as how to tap their creativity--that are vital in all fields of learning and professional activities. Any educational system deserving the name should cultivate creativity in students. Creativity is an inspired, expressive behavior; it comes in flashes and furor; it is a product of fascination and inventiveness, of inner exploration, and self-discovery. Creativity requires the ability to listen and follow inner impulses or voices that speak to what is right and wrong. Only a system based on intrinsic learning will develop the students' ability to realize their creativity as they confront problems. Creativity can neither be taught by operant conditioning nor it will ensue as a product of method. Method is a technique in which non-creative people create. Arts and music education, as against critical thinking and method, for example, offer intuitive glimpses into inner values and should be the paradigm for all fields of education in which students learn to express themselves creatively. Once intrinsically acquainted with their creativity, students will learn how to reach for and release it in their self-chosen vocational fields. And, like creativity, Maslow noted, there are other skills necessary in all fields of learning. Experts in any field should be comfortable and enjoy change, be able to improvise, and face situations that emerge without warning with confidence, strength, and courage.[17]

We should not, however, argued Maslow, devalue specific professional skills and knowledge of various disciplines. It is not enough just to be creative and intrinsically willing to become a civil engineer. Concrete knowledge of engineering, mathematics, and physics is also a prerequisite. The ideal, thus, was to integrate intrinsic learning with traditional extrinsic learning, such as training of professional skills or education for competence in any field. The main difference was whether this knowledge is sought out of personal need and meaning or as a response to rewarding or punishing stimuli. Knowledge gathered out of personal meaning translates into a lasting expressive behavior that is independent of reinforcing external stimuli.[18]

Rogers' Student-Centered Learning

Rogers' views on education were an outgrowth of his client-centered therapy, more precisely, the concept of "significant learning." Significant learning in client-centered therapy penetrates the whole character structure of the individual, deeply changing his or her mode of being. When this type of learning occurs in psychotherapy, the patient's self-image and feelings improve and realistic goals and mature behavior are adopted. The patient thus develops a better awareness of inner and outer worlds. Rogers postulated that the therapist must provide five necessary and sufficient conditions in order for significant learning to occur. The first condition is the congruence of the therapist's relationship with the client. By congruence, Rogers meant awareness and expression of what the therapist is experiencing in the relationship. In other words, the therapist is perceived as an integrated and authentic person, not a facade or role. The second condition is the therapist's free expression and acceptance of his or her own immediate feelings. The third condition is the therapist's expression of a caring warmth for the client as a person in his or her own right, thus providing a secure climate of "unconditional positive regard." By unconditional positive regard, Rogers meant the therapist's acceptance of the client's expression of negative or "bad" and positive or "good" feelings without evaluating these feelings. In this sense, the client is given permission to express and find meaning in his or her own feelings. The fourth condition states that the therapist must experience an accurate empathic understanding of the client's private world--his or her anger, fear and confusion, as if these were the therapist's own feelings. This condition in turn enables the therapist to reflect back to the client his or her understanding of what is already known, thus awakening the client to the meanings he or she is scarcely aware of. The fifth and final condition is the ability of the therapist to communicate to the client his or her own congruence, acceptance and empathy. When these five conditions are met, significant learning induces a constructive process of personality change and growth. The reason this occurs, wrote Rogers, is that when the organism is integrated and allowed free and authentic expression, it releases a "self-actualizing tendency" to grow and fulfill all its potential.[19]

When Rogers applied this reasoning to education, he argued that if significant learning is to occur in the classroom, the teacher, like the therapist, must create a climate that facilitates the realization of these same five conditions. Rogers also pointed out that in education, like in therapy, it is essential that the student is curious, explorative, in touch with the problem, and conscious that its solution has personal significance. If the student lives through the problem and the five necessary and sufficient conditions are met, an astonishing amount of significant learning takes place.[20]

The first implication of Rogers' ideas in psychotherapy when applied to education is the realness of the teacher. The teacher is not supposed to be a mere "faceless embodiment of a curricular requirement," or a "sterile pipe" through which knowledge is transmitted, but rather a congruent person, authentic in the classroom, who accepts and manifests his or her feelings. Secondly, the teacher must warmly accept, understand, and empathize with the student in his or her own terms; and, among other things, the teacher must unconditionally accept the student's feelings of fear and discouragement which are always present when learning something new. Thirdly, the instructional resources must be readily available, but never forced upon the student. The teacher should let the students know that his or her personal knowledge is available to them in whatever form they want, whether in a lecture format or as a resource-finder. The student will not perceive the learning experience as the teacher's expectations, commands, impositions or requirements. The task of the teacher is merely to facilitate the student's satisfaction of his or her own intellectual curiosity.[21]

Conclusion

Although most educators in the late 1950s and 1960s had read Skinner's *Walden Two* (1948) and other education-related writings, Skinner's impact on education was insignificant. The radical behavioristic educational program was, in general terms, regarded as a utopia, indeed, a fearful utopia for some. The teaching-machines and the cast of social technicians failed to relate to the human aspects of education. It was absurd to treat children as behaving organisms to be educated along the lines of control and prediction of behavior used in studies of rats, pigeons and apes. But in an age that overestimated the social applications of science, the scientism inherent in behaviorism and the concrete application of behavioral techniques as tools in occupational therapy and other more extreme behavioral disabilities represented powerful arguments against a more humanistic approach toward teachers education. Torn between the scientific credibility of behaviorism and the human realities of the classroom, educators during the 1960s, a time when the so-called counter-culture had stirred an unprecedented openness to new ideas, were ready for an alternative philosophy.

Not surprisingly, the humanistic paradigm in education was by the 1970s firmly established. Today, most, if not all, educators have a notion of

Rogers' student-centered education and Maslow's intrinsic learning and expressive behavior. Both Rogers and Maslow reawakened educators to the need to humanize education and, in doing so, helped to dismantle the monopoly enjoyed by behaviorism in the American social sciences of the mid-20th century.

The growth hypothesis of Kurt Goldstein was a source of inspiration for Rogers and Maslow, whose studies on self-actualization served as a breeding ground for the establishment of the humanistic movement in American psychology. Their interpretations of the growth hypothesis also dictated their understanding of human nature, naturalistic ethics, and the humanistic paradigm in education.

Their views on education stemmed from a basic trust of the worthiness of human nature. They argued that when people are authentic, experience their inner worlds, and function free from internal and external barriers, they will value and choose (from an organismic point of view) what is good for them. "To be that self which one truly is," a phrase Rogers borrowed from Kierkegaard that is synonymous with the seeking of authenticity, was the highest value in Rogers and Maslow's naturalistic system of ethics. In Maslow's words, authenticity was "truthfulness to one's own nature." The goal of education, they thought, was to teach students to discover and utilize to the maximum their organismic potential and wisdom.

Although two-decades old, Maslow and Rogers' humanistic message is still valid for the 1990s. The success of any educational system depends on its ability to involve students in the process of learning and to perceive meaning in the acquisition of knowledge. Without the student's wonder, curiosity, and personal need to learn, good teachers and well-funded schools will fail. Students are not merely rat-like response organisms that learn technological knowledge and skills in response to rewarding stimuli. According to Maslow and Rogers, students learn only when they seek to actualize their inner human potential. The teacher should thus make an alliance with the student's natural curiosity and organismic forces pressing for growth and facilitate the process of self-discovery, so that the student may find the vocation and skills he or she is intrinsically suited for. Once this alliance has been made it is also the educator's responsibility to make extrinsic knowledge available and teach specific skills. Teachers themselves should serve as a role model of people who are authentic, curious, explorative, and perplexed by the wonders of their disciplines.

ENDNOTES

[1] Maslow, (Ed.), *New Knowledge in Human Values* (New York: Harper, 1959), pp. viii, 119-136; *Religion, Values and Peak-Experiences* (Columbus: Ohio State University Press, 1964), pp. 3,38,82; *Farther Reaches of Human Nature* (New York: Viking, 1971), p. 377. Rogers, "The Developing Values of the Growing Person," *The Psychiatric Institute Bulletin* (University of Wisconsin) 1 (1961): 1-15; "Toward a Modern Approach to Values: The Valuing Process in the Mature Person," *Journal of Abnormal Social Psychology* 68 (1964): 160-167; R. I. Evans, *Carl Rogers: The Man and His Ideas* (New York: Dutton, 1975), p. 101.

[2] Maslow, *Religion, Values and Peak-Experiences*, p. 49. Rogers, *The Developing Values*; "Toward a Modern Approach"; Evans, *Rogers*, p. 101.

[3] Maslow, "Eupsychia-The Good Society," *Journal of Humanistic Psychology*, 1 (1961): 1-11; *Farther Reaches*, pp. 168-179,180-195; "Farther Reaches of Human Nature," *Journal of Humanistic Psychology* 1 (1968): 1-9; "Conversation with Abraham H. Maslow. *Psychology Today* 2 (1968): 34-37,54-57; "Goals in Humanistic Education," in *Esalen Papers* (Big Sur: Esalen Institute, 1968). Rogers, "A Therapist View of the Good Life, *The Humanist* 17 (1957): 291-300; *To Be That Self Which One Truly Is: A Therapist's View of Personal Goals* (Transcript of a Talk at the College of Wooster, Ohio, on March 14, 1957); "The Developing Values"; "Toward a Modern Approach."

[4] Maslow, *Motivation and Personality* (New York: Harper, 1954); R. J. DeCarvalho, "Abraham H. Maslow (1908-1970): An Intellectual Biography," *Thought: Review of Culture and Idea* 66 (1991); E. Hoffman, *The Right to be*

Human: A Biography of Abraham Maslow (Los Angeles: Jeremy P. Tarcher, 1988).

[5] Rogers, "Personal Thoughts on Teaching and Learning," *Merrill-Palmer Quarterly* 3 (1957): 241-243; "Significant Learning: In Therapy and in Education," *Educational Leadership* 16 (1959): 232-242; "The Facilitation of Significant Learning," in L. Siegel (Ed.), *Contemporary Theories of Instruction* (San Francisco: Chandler, 1967), pp. 37-54; "The Interpersonal Relationship in the Facilitation of Learning," in R. Leeper (Ed.), *Humanizing Education* (National Education Association for Supervision and Curriculum Development, 1967), pp. 1-18.

[6] Rogers, "A Plan for Self-directed Change in an Educational System," *Educational Leadership* 24 (1967): 717-731; "A Practical Plan for Educational Revolution," In R. R. Goulet (Ed.), *Educational Change: The Reality and the Promise, a Report on the National Seminar on Innovation* (New York: Citation Press, 1968); "The Project at Immaculate Heart: An Experiment in Self-Directed Change," *Education* 95 (1974): 172-196.

[7] Rogers, *Freedom to Learn: A View of What Education Might Become* (Columbus: Merrill, 1969); "Can Schools Grow Persons," *Educational Leadership* 29 (1971): 215-217; "Forget You Are a Teacher. Carl Rogers Tells Why," *Instructor*, August/September 1971, 65-66; "Bringing Together Ideas and Feelings in Learning," *Learning Today* 5, (1972): 32-43; "Questions I Would Ask Myself If I Were a Teacher," *Education* 95 (1974): 134-139.

[8] R. J. DeCarvalho, *The Founders of Humanistic Psychology* (New York: Praeger, 1991), chap. 4; B. F. Skinner, *Walden Two* (New York: MacMillan, 1948); "The Science of Learning and the Art of Teaching," *Harvard Educational Review* 24 (1954): 84-97; "Why we Need Teaching Machines," *Harvard Educational Review* 31 (1961): 377-398.

[9] Rogers, "Personal Thoughts"; Significant Learning"; *Freedom to Learn*. Maslow, *Farther Reaches*, pp. 168-179; "Goals in Humanistic Education"; "Humanistic Education vs. Professional Education," *New Directions in Teaching* 2 (1969): 6-8.

[10] Rogers, "A Personal View of Some Issues Facing Psychologists," *American Psychologist* 10 (1955): 247-249; *On Becoming a Person* (Boston: Houghton Mifflin, 1961), p. 391. Maslow, *Motivation and Personality*, pp. 6-12; "A Philosophy of Psychology," in F. T. Severin (Ed.), *Humanistic Viewpoints in Psychology* (New York: McGraw-Hill, 1956), pp. 17-33; *Toward a*

Psychology of Being (New York: Nostrand, 1962), chap. 1, pp. 189-214; Evans, *Rogers*, p. 101; W. B. Frick, *Humanistic Psychology: Interview with Maslow, Murphy and Rogers* (Columbus: Merrill, 1971), pp. 22-32.

[11] Rogers, "Significant Learning"; "The Facilitation of Significant Learning"; "Beyond the Watershed in Education," *Teaching-Learning Journal*, Winter/Spring 1976, 43-49; "Beyond the Watershed: And Where Now?" *Educational Leadership* 34 (1977): 623-631. Maslow, *Motivation and Personality*, p. 111; "Some Frontier Problems," p. 8; "Goals in Humanistic Education"; *Farther Reaches*, pp. 180-195.

[12] Maslow, *Motivation and Personality*, p. 111; "Some Frontier Problems," p. 8; "Goals in Humanistic Education." Rogers, "Personal Thoughts"; "Significant Learning"; "The Facilitation of Significant Learning."

[13] Maslow, *Religion, Values and Peak-Experiences*; *Farther Reaches*, pp. 180-195. Rogers, "Significant Learning"; "Toward a Modern Approach"; "The Facilitation of Significant Learning"; "The Formative Tendency," *Journal of Humanistic Psychology* 18 (1978): 23-26; Frick, *Humanistic Psychology*, p. 33.

[14] Maslow, *Motivation and Personality*, pp. 103, 179-198,291; *Farther Reaches*, 168-179; "Humanistic Education."

[15] Maslow, *Motivation and Personality*, pp. 179-198; "Goals in Humanistic Education."

[16] Maslow, *The Psychology of Science*, pp. 40-44.

[17] Maslow, *Farther Reaches*, pp. 57-61,99-101,168-179; "Goals in Humanistic Education."

[18] Maslow, "Humanistic Education"; "Humanistic Education vs. Professional Education: Further Comments"; *New Directions in Teaching* 2 (1970): 3-10.

[19] Rogers, *Client-Centered Therapy*; "The Necessary and Sufficient Conditions of Therapeutic Personality Change," *Journal of Consulting Psychology* 21 (1957): 95-103; "Significant Learning."

[20] Rogers, "The Necessary and Sufficient Conditions"; "Can School Grow Persons?"; "Bringing Together Ideas and Feelings"; "Can Learning Encompass Both Ideas and Feelings?," *Education* 95 (1974): 103-114.

[21] Rogers, "The Facilitation of Significant Learning"; "Beyond the Watershed."

Chapter 6

ON THE PROBLEM OF METHOD IN PSYCHOLOGY

Although a positivist methodology permeates most studies of human nature by American psychologists, it would be overly parochial to fail to recognize that in the non-English speaking world the existential and phenomenological perspective prevails.

Seen from a Western perspective, 20th century psychology has been dominated by the experimental, or objective, and the experiential, or subjective, paradigms of human nature and method. According to the objective paradigm, human nature is a natural phenomenon to be studied by the methods of the natural sciences. The positivist philosophy, proposed by Auguste Comte at the beginning of the nineteenth century, was the first clear enunciation of this view in the social sciences. Comte assumed that physical, biological, human, and social phenomena were equal in nature, and he advocated the introduction of the positivist method to the human sciences.[1]

Comte's program was taken up a century later by experimental psychologists who advocated the exclusive use of observation in the study of human behavior. Throughout the first half of the twentieth century, behaviorism perpetuated Comte's ideal. J. B. Watson, founder of the science of behavior, thought that since there was no dividing line between people and animals, both could be studied with equal success under the same experimental conditions. Watson thus proposed a psychology that was a "purely objective experimental branch of natural sciences," an approach that was reflected most significantly in the work of B. F. Skinner.[2]

During the first quarter of the 20th century, the German phenomenologist Edmund Husserl criticized this positivistic or "psychologism" attitude. He thought that humans have a subjective form of existence, the study of which requires the development of a unique science, not an imitation of the natural science model. In 1925, Husserl termed his new science "phenomenological psychology," or the science of inner-experience, subjectivity, and the mental.[3]

A decade later, reacting against Husserl's transcendental phenomenological philosophy and concept of the transcendental ego, Martin Heidegger and Jean-Paul Sartre argued that Husserl had gone too far in the search for transcendental concepts within subjectivity, thus betraying his own phenomenological principles. By requesting a return to subjectivity, they created an existentialist wing within the phenomenological movement. Sartre proposed an existential psychoanalysis of his own, and Ludwig Binswanger and Medard Boss, elaborating on Heidegger's concept of Dasein, developed the Daseinsanalysis.[4]

Since Husserl's criticism of psychologism, the positivistic ideal of experimental psychology has been considered philosophically immature by phenomenological and existential psychologists, whose studies of consciousness and subjectivity have in turn been viewed by experimental psychologists as rather esoteric pursuits. Proponents of both paradigms accuse one another of naively misunderstanding human nature and the methodology of psychology. Seen from a non-parochial perspective, this is the most dramatic issue in the history of psychology. American psychology, however, has had the privilege of clarification between the experimental and experiential paradigms offered in the work of the humanistic psychologists.[5]

Maslow and Rogers wrote eloquently on the philosophical tension between these paradigms as they applied to the study of both the objective and subjective components of human nature. In fact, no other American psychologists since William James personally lived the tension and understood the two paradigms better than they did.[6]

This chapter examines Maslow and Rogers' contributions on the problem of method in psychology. Their theoretical standpoint is particularly suitable to the clarification of the philosophical tension between the two psychological paradigms since they introduced their understanding of phenomenology and existentialism into the very heart of the positivistic milieu that intellectually nurtured them. Like their humanistic colleagues, they knew and identified with both methodologies.

Rogers' Quantitative Studies in Psychotherapy

Early in Rogers' career, he acknowledged that psychotherapy combines artistry with science and that experiential, not cognitive, learning is essential in training therapists. The proliferation, however, of unchecked theories and techniques had created a state of chaos, making psychotherapy a cult of personalities and systems. This situation, he argued, made inevitable the development of fact-finding empirical attitudes, objective measurements, and appraisals of the basic experiential and subjective aspects of psychotherapy. There was a need to clarify the goals of psychotherapy, evaluate outcomes, measure success and failure, validate theoretical assumptions, and determine what is a healing and what is a destructive experience. Adopting Thorndike's dictum that "anything that exists, exists in some quantity that can be measured," Rogers argued that if psychotherapeutic skills and the psychological processes they initiated can be observed in practical clinical experience, then experimental conditions can be developed that will measure, prove, disprove, or modify scientific hypotheses.[7]

Rogers' raw data in the quantification of psychotherapeutic processes were gathered as phonographically recorded interviews. He was the first to employ the then new audio recording technology in psychological research. His *Counseling and Psychotherapy* (1942) presented for the first time a complete verbatim account of a successful counseling case study. Snyders' *Case Book of Non-Directive Counseling* (1947) presented five additional cases. By the early 1950s, Rogers had recorded and transcribed eighty more cases at the Counseling Center of the University of Chicago. Based on these verbatim case-studies, Rogers and his associates measured the changes in personality structure and behavior, the increase in attitudes of acceptance toward oneself and others, and the decrease in psychological tension that occurred in psychotherapy.[8]

Rogers showed that in a field noted more for its art than its science, non-directive psychotherapy provided a simple, clear and consistent hypothesis of the if-then type of invariance, with an operational definition given to experimental testing. If the necessary and sufficient conditions are fulfilled, then there is a predictable chain of events. More precisely, if the therapist is congruent in the relationship with the client and provides unconditional positive regard and empathy for the client's condition, then significant and constructive personality changes will occur. Since all the factors in the equation could be measured, Rogers and his associates at Ohio State University and the University of Chicago tested this hypothesis.[9]

Clients at the Counseling Center were given the traditional batteries of personality tests (primarily the Rorschach, Kent-Rosanoff Word Association, Thematic Apperception Test, and Bell Adjustment Inventory) and the Q-sort test. The tests measured various personality characteristics of clients before the first interview, two months later at the beginning of therapy, after its completion, and at a follow-up point six months to one year later.[10]

The Q-sort test implemented by William Stephenson of the Chicago Center was developed from the Q-technique of Victor Raimy, a close associate of Rogers at Ohio State University. The analysis of self-descriptive statements drawn from the recorded interviews led to a sampling of 100 edited and unambiguous statements of ways people perceive themselves. The statements were classified into positive, negative, and ambivalent categories. Printed on cards, the statements were given to a client who chose the cards that most accurately describe him or her and represent the self he or she would like to be, e.g., the ideal self.[11]

Administered at different stages in the process of therapy, the client's Q-sort, the traditional personality tests, and the Q-sort analyses of the patient's recorded interviews by independent observers showed that there were alterations in the person's concept of self, thus confirming the basic hypothesis of the client-centered approach, e.g, that changes in the picture of oneself--one's "internal frame of reference"--have a profound influence on personality and behavioral changes. Rogers also concluded that the perceived self-image of the client changes more during therapy than during a period of no therapy, that the perceived self is more positively valued after therapy, and is more congruent with the ideal, or valued self. After a successful therapy, self-confidence, self-reliance, self-understanding, inner comfort, and more satisfying relationships with others increase, while feelings of guilt, resentment, and insecurity decrease.[12]

Maslow's Studies in Comparative Psychology

Like Rogers, Maslow too made his reputation in psychology through quantitative studies, first of primates and later of New York City college women. Maslow first encountered experimental psychology, behaviorism in particular, as a philosophy student at Cornell. His dislike of the speculative character of philosophical discourse attracted him to the empirical and physiological 19th century psychology advocated in America by Tichener. The discovery of Watson's behavioristic program, he noted many years later, left a deep impression. The techniques of conditioning promised a solution to all psychological and social problems, while its easy-to-understand positivistic, objective philosophy he believed protected him from repeating the philo-sophical mistakes of the past. With such ideas in mind, Maslow joined the Department of Psychology at the University of Wisconsin-Madison, where in the primate laboratory of Harry Harlow he was nurtured in the best behav-ioristic tradition of the 1930s. Here he received a BA (1930), MA (1931) and PhD (1934) in psychology. Thus great familiarity with experimental psychol-ogy, behaviorism in particular, is evident in his critique of this model of psychological science.[13]

Maslow's research at the University of Wisconsin-Madison focused on classical laboratory research with dogs and apes. His MA thesis, an experi-mental study of the effect of varying simple external conditions in learning, initiated him into the science of prediction and control of behavior. His doctoral dissertation explored the role of dominance in the social and sexual behavior of primates, arguing that dominance among primates is usually established by visual contact rather than by fighting.[14]

Maslow's transition from the study of apes to the study of humans can be traced to his encounter with Alfred Adler soon after his departure from Madison. Adler read Maslow's dissertation on the social behavior of pri-mates and encouraged him to write a summary for the *Journal of Individual Psychology*. Maslow's essay indirectly invited comparisons between the behav-ior of humans and apes by placing an asterisk next to statements about apes that had a close human parallel. "It remains true," he wrote, "now as always, that in the animal, it seems, we see ourselves writ small and clear."[15] Since humans are animals themselves, there was hope, he argued, that the study of animals will help us understand ourselves. He thus advocated experimental studies of human subjects employing control groups of apes. The recourse to apes, he argued, simplified the problems and development of experimental apparatus in the study of humans, giving him definite hints, hypotheses, methods and objective criteria by which to judge human behavior.[16]

Maslow's research in comparative psychology focused on the relationship between dominance and sexual behavior and their correlation to self-esteem, both from a biological and a cultural point of view. He concluded that sexual attitudes and behavior were more closely related to personal and social dominance than to sexual drive. The only difference between apes and humans was in the extent of internalization of social inhibitions present in humans. In the late 1930s, however, Maslow gradually lost all interest in apes and concentrated on the study of female college students. He developed experimental studies and inventories in social personality that measured the correlation between feelings of security, self-esteem, and social and sexual dominance. Maslow's suspicion that these human conditions are key components in the presence or absence of mental health turned into a life-long interest in the study of the psychologically healthy personality. Maslow's last experimental study measured the effects of beauty and ugliness, more specifically, the short term effects on people of three visual aesthetic conditions--"beautiful," "average," and "ugly."[17]

Maslow's Psychology of Health and Growth

A year after graduation, however, Maslow left behind the behavioristic approach of his teachers. In New York City, while teaching at Teacher's College, Columbia University, and Brooklyn College, Maslow read Freud, the Gestalt psychologists, and the embryologist Ludwig von Bertalanffy. During this period Maslow also became disillusioned with English philosophy, particularly as represented by Bertrand Russell. During World War II, when a number of exiled German psychologists made New York City their home, Maslow associated with Alfred Adler, Max Wertheimer, Erich Fromm, Karen Horney, Kurt Goldstein, and Ruth Benedict. It was under their influence that Maslow shifted the focus of his experimental studies of dominance and sexual behavior from primates to humans. It was in the context of this research that Maslow developed his well-known theory of human motivation.[18]

As soon as Maslow began studying human subjects in the late 1930s, he recognized that psychological research and personality theories relied almost exclusively on subjects who had turned to psychologists for pathological reasons. The view of human nature stemming from the study of the illnesses of these patients was inevitably distorted and pessimistic. "The study of crippled stunted, immature, and unhealthy specimens," he wrote, "can yield a cripple psychology and a crippled philosophy." In this context Maslow criticized orthodox psychologists for studying and formulating their views on human nature on the basis of primarily pathological human subjects.[19]

Physiological and psychological health in the orthodox view was defined as the mere absence of illness, the relief of symptoms, or the cessation of any particular kind of misery. It meant the transformation of acute misery into normal suffering. Trying to remedy the situation, Maslow selected for study a small sample of the healthiest people he could find, a panel of students representing about one percent of the college population.[20]

Maslow's original criteria for "health" were the absence of neurosis, psychosis, and other symptoms of abnormal personality. In determining these, he employed the Rorschach and other traditional personality tests, and conducted extensive clinical interviews, looking for evidence of self-actualization, such as the full use and exploitation of talents, capacities, potentialities, and the gratification of basic emotional needs: safety, belonging, and love. He wanted to know more about the higher levels of human nature, what qualities and values induce health and self-esteem, and what was the significance of those all-too human qualities that were poetic, mythic, and symbolic in nature.[21]

This pioneering study of psychological health obviously posed many problems, and Maslow had to develop new methods, concepts, and attitudes. In the first major work presenting this research, Maslow apologized to those who insisted on conventional reliability, validity and procedural standards for the methodological shortcomings of the research. He described his attempt as a primitive naturalistic and phenomenological pilot study, a private venture motivated by his own curiosity in which he sought to learn rather than prove or demonstrate.[22]

In doing so Maslow believed that he had initiated a revolution in psychology, creating a new Zeitgeist or humanistic Weltanschaung in the principles and methods of the human sciences. Colin Wilson concurred with Maslow's estimation of his own work. Wilson placed Maslow among the most original and influential thinkers in post-Freudian psychology.[23]

Rogers on Subjective Knowledge

While Maslow came to study the subjective aspect of psychology through the study of psychological health, Rogers, on the other hand, began studying the subjective aspects of psychotherapy primarily as a result of the existentialist ideas of Soren Kierkegaard and Martin Buber, which he became familiar with in the late 1950s.[24]

While in Chicago Rogers became increasingly torn between the tenets of logical positivism and subjectivism. Prompted by the insistence of some theology students taking his classes, Rogers read the writings of Buber and Kierkegaard. This reading had a "loosening up" effect upon him, encouraging him to trust and write about his own subjective experiences in the practice of psychotherapy. He thought that their insights and convictions expressed views he had held, but had been unable to formulate.[25]

One of these insights was Kierkegaard's statement that the aim of life is "to be that self which one truly is." Rogers interpreted the passage to mean that the most common despair results from not being responsible for becoming what one truly is, but rather desiring to be something else. This idea had been a cornerstone of Rogers' thought on the self and person-centered psychotherapy. Rogers agreed with Kierkegaard that the goal of life was to move away from "oughts" and facades. In therapy, argued Rogers, when a person becomes what he or she inwardly is, then the inner messages and meanings of the self will be heard. When this happens, a deep desire to be fully oneself in all one's complexity and richness follows, withholding and fearing nothing that is part of the inner self. Self-experience becomes a friendly resource and not a frightening enemy.[26]

The thinking of the Hasidic philosopher, Martin Buber, also influenced Rogers in that he thought, in addition to "unconditional positive regard," and the immediacy and realness of the therapist, a deep sense of communication and unity between the therapist and the client was crucial. In this sense, therapy was a genuine person-to-person experience, which was exactly what Buber had described in the "I-thou relationship." Buber thought that the deep mutual experience of speaking truly to one another without playing a "role," e.g., the meeting between two persons at a deep and significant level, had a healing effect. Buber named this process, "healing through meeting." It was this process that Rogers experienced in the most effective moments of psychotherapy.[27]

Describing the essence of therapy in terms of his personal experience, Rogers explained that when he entered the therapeutic relationship he made a sincere and gradually unconscious attempt to understand and unconditionally accept the inner world of the other as a subject. He had faith that in doing so a significant personality change would follow, which, in turn, would foster a more authentic and satisfying process of becoming in the client. People come to therapy because they have grown alienated from their true selves and thus lost contact with their organismic wisdom. The therapist's unconditional acceptance and interest in the inner self of the client invites him or her to follow the therapist's steps. In this process there is unity of experiencing, a trance-like situation in which both therapist and client slip together into a stream of subjective authentic becoming. A real "I-thou" relationship, as Buber described, is the height of personal subjectivity.[28]

It is easy for the therapist to engage in this process because he has lived the experience many times, but as the client begins to recognize its healing effect he or she follows the role model of the therapist and learns to explore the healing potential of the intimate encounter. Once people learn to dip into their subjectivity and the intimacy of the therapeutic encounter, there is a gradual growth of trust and even affection for the awareness of their organismic wisdom. This is a sort of learning or process of self-discovery that cannot be taught, it can only be experienced subjectively. Only true subjective understanding will make this type of learning possible. Even when learned it cannot be symbolized or intellectually recreated. It has value and immediacy only when experienced. Once experienced it also has a significant life-lasting effect.

Rogers' Three Modes of Knowing

At first, Rogers understood the experimental and experiential as two legitimate approaches to the study of psychotherapy, each holding significant truths, but they are antagonistic and irreconcilable points of view. He wrote about this conflict "between the logical empiricism in which I was educated, for which I had a deep respect, and the subjectively oriented existential thinking which was taking root in me because it seemed to fit so well with my therapeutic experience."[30]

By the mid-sixties, however, Rogers solved this conflict within himself. He proposed a new science of human nature, e.g. humanistic psychology, integrating the objective and subjective modes of knowing with a third mode, the intersubjective or phenomenological mode. Rogers sought a non-mechanistic model of science developed from an existential orientation, but preserving the values of logical positivism and placing the subjective person at the very heart of the system. He argued from the outset that there were three modes of knowing, the subjective or experiential, the objective or experimental, and a synthesis of the two, which he named interpersonal or phenomenological knowing.[31]

Subjective knowledge ensues from experience and the internal frame of reference of the person. Love, hate, joy, and similar subjective judgments are personal, inner hypotheses that have meaning only in relation to our internal frame of reference. The sharper, more precise, and accurate we are in relation to our inner and outer realities, the more correct also our subjective hypothesis will be. In psychotherapy, for example, one often searches for words and hypothesis that more accurately describe inner experiences, feelings, and ways of being. There is often a great sense of relief when specific knowledge of the inner self replaces vague knowing. In psychotherapy one often contradicts previously held hypothesis due to the increase in self-knowledge: the criterion is always the internal frame of reference of the person and the stream of experiencing the world.[32]

Although fundamental in everyday living, subjective knowledge is just that, subjective. It has little or no significance except for the person, and for this reason modern psychological science has had little regard for it. When, however, we test our inner hypothesis with other people or in an objective assessment, then, Rogers argued, we seek intersubjective verification that leads us to the domain of objective knowledge.[33]

Objective knowledge relies upon an external frame of reference, observable events and operations. When independent observers who speak the same language, share similar values and a contextual framework, collect, examine, and test data, they arrive at similar conclusions and assume that such knowledge is independent of the observer, and thus objective. This method, according to Rogers, is restricted only to observable facts. It also transforms whatever it studies into objects to be manipulated and dissected.[34]

The interpersonal or phenomenological knowledge, Rogers' third mode of knowing, is a synthesis of the objective and subjective methods. In this mode, there is an attempt to objectively know the subjective hypothesis of the phenomenological frame of reference of a person by whatever available means. The goal is to penetrate the private world of the person and test the validity of the therapist's--and the client's--hypotheses in relation to his or her internal frame of reference. The simpler, but not always accurate, way to achieve this is to ask the person specific questions or observe his or her behavior. In client-centered therapy, the counselor creates a psychological climate in which it is safe and rewarding for the person to reveal the internal frame of reference, against which the therapist's and the client's own hypotheses may hopefully be validated.[35]

Rogers argued that people and scientists do not use only one mode exclusively. We all trust to some extent our experience of the world and intuition about people. Most of us also test our subjective knowledge with those or about those we care in empathic and phenomenological ways. Some of us even put our hypothesis to the most severe tests in the objective world and remain open either to the confirmation or denial of our tentative hypothesis.

Maslow's Taoistic Method in Psychology

Maslow had similar thoughts on the problem of method in psychology, describing Rogers' phenomenological process of knowing as a taoistic science.[36]

In *The Psychology of Science* (1966), originally an invitational lecture of the John Dewey Society, Maslow elaborated on the philosophy of psychology first argued in *Motivation and Personality* (1954). The chapter on "Taoistic Science" presented original thoughts on phenomenology and the problem of method in psychology. He described taoistic knowledge as an approach to learning meant to complement Western science. He argued that the organization, classification, and conceptualization methods of Western science removed our perception of reality to an abstract realm invented by the mind. This negative orientation should be balanced against a taoistic, non-intruding receptivity and contemplation of experience, or "getting back to things them-selves," as Husserl had argued. He referred to this type of knowledge as "taoistic objectivity," as opposed to "classical objectivity."[37]

Maslow had no doubts that the psychologists' attempts to imitate out-dated models of the physical sciences had only depersonalized psychology, turning it into an atomistic and mechanistic science. A science of human nature in which the observer is also the observed has to be a unique science. Maslow recognized that the empiricism of logical positivism and the private subjective world of existential mysticism should be balanced and proposed a philosophy of psychology that synthesized both methods. Like Rogers, he also termed the new endeavor--humanistic psychology.[38]

Maslow argued that all knowledge is a product of experience. At some point in the process of experience, one senses the emergence of a pattern, rhythm, or relationship. "Some things just come to mind," wrote Maslow. He learned that when the organism operates freely and non-defensively, it is able to sense a pattern even before it can consciously formulate it. But this sensing is not enough. By itself it is as unacceptable as the rigidity of a behavioral psychologist. The subjective hypothesis ought to be first put to a rough test, and then confirmed, modified, or disproved in more rigorous testing. Arguing that there is no special virtue in any particular testing procedure, Maslow thought that the method of testing should be appropriate to the nature of the hypothesis. The statistical method, for example, should not be used to test the phenomenon of subjectivity.[39]

Maslow's discussion of "taoistic science" addressed the significance of phenomenological knowledge. All knowledge pertaining to human life must first be known by direct and intimate experience. There is no substitute for experience. Conceptual, abstract, theoretical knowledge is useful only when people already know experientially. Words fail when there is no experience and succeed when people share similar experiences.[40]

These first efforts in psychological research are inelegant, imprecise,

and crude. They require honest and authentic knowing, surrender, identification, and unselfish fusion with the object under study; they require those
involved to observe, listen, absorb, without presupposing, classifying, improving, evaluating, or approving. It assumes fearless respect for the object as it is
and suspension of judgment. The psychologist should relax, let it go, melt
away with the object of study, experience it receptively, taoistically and
contemplatively, not intruding or interfering with the order of things.

Maslow described this first stage as "taoistic nonintruding receptivity to
the experience." In other words, it is more an attitude than a technique. At
this level of study experience just happens as it is and not according to the
psychologist's expectations of control and prediction. As researchers, however, begin to organize, classify, and abstract their phenomenological accounts
of the object under study, they move away from reality as it is and begin to
document it as their own hypothetical constructions determine their perception of experience.[41]

Toward a More Humanistic Psychology

Rogers and Maslow had no doubt that the attempt by psychologists' to
imitate what they thought were outdated models of the physical sciences had
only made psychology mechanistic and depersonalized. A science of human
nature in which the observer is also the observed had to be a unique science.
Thus, recognizing the need for a balance between the empiricism of positivistic psychology and the private, subjective world of existential mysticism,
Rogers and Maslow developed a philosophy and methodology of science that
combined quantitative and phenomenological methods and recognized the
centrality of human subjectivity--a rare achievement indeed in the history and
systems of psychology. They termed the new endeavor, humanistic psychology.[42]

In their proposal for a psychology humanistic in nature, Maslow and

Rogers argued, like the Continental phenomenologists and existentialists, that psychological research should begin with a "getting back to the things themselves." Study of human nature should begin with phenomenological knowledge and only then be submitted to objective, experimental, and behavioral laboratory methods of study.

Specifically addressing the then in vogue behavioristic psychology, Rogers and Maslow argued that exclusive focus on external behavior, disregard for the rich world of personal meanings, and avoidance of subjectivity place the human being in the same line of ontological existence as rats and pigeons. The whole range of human experience, the existential world of the person, they argued, should be taken into consideration. In doing so, they were confident that humanistic psychology would invigorate the field of psychology by broadening the restrictive scope of psychology as the study of control and prediction of behavior. Rogers and Maslow thus believed they were laying the seeds of a newer philosophy of psychology which was not fearful of studying the person, who happens to be both the observer and the observed, in his or her subjective as well as objective existence. Humanistic psychology would open psychology to all significant human problems and utilize all channels of knowing.[43]

Rogers, for example, argued that all knowledge is a product of experiencing, thus rewriting the Cartesian dictum as "I experience--therefore I exist." "All knowledge, including all scientific knowledge," he wrote, "is a vast inverted pyramid resting on this tiny, personal, subjective base."[44] When one studies human nature, one should trust one's intuition and be guided by the experiences that subjectively move us to question, be perplexed and study that particular phenomenon. One should, thus, first and foremost immerse and experience from within the particular human phenomenon one is studying. One should be open to all subtleties of experience, tolerate ambiguity and contradiction. One should, in other words, be personally involved in what one is studying. Truly "indwell" in the feelings, attitudes and perceptions of

those being studied and the data collected. In Rogers' words, "it means soaking up experience like a sponge so that it is taken in all its complexity, with
my total organism freely participating in the experiencing of the phenomena,
not simply my conscious mind."[45] Maslow termed this attitude "taoistic receptivity."

At some point in the process of "soaking up experience" or "taoistic
receptivity" Maslow and Rogers similarly argued that one senses the emergence of a pattern, rhythm or relationship. "Some things just come to mind,"
they argued.[46] They were confident that when one operates freely and non-
defensively one is able to sense a pattern even before one can consciously
formulate it. But this sensing is not enough. By itself it is as unacceptable as
is the rigidity of a behavioral psychologist. The subjective hypothesis ought to
be put first to a rough test, and later, to rigorous testing that will confirm,
modify or disconfirm it. Arguing that there is no special virtue in any particular testing procedure, they thought that the method of testing should be
appropriate to the nature of the hypothesis.

Maslow and Rogers, however, never totally denied the value of quantitative methods in the human sciences. The experiential and experimental
modes of knowing, they argued, are not dichotomously antagonist; it is not
the case of experience versus abstracting; cautious versus bold knowledge.
Both forms complement each other. Abstract knowledge dichotomized from
experiential knowledge is dangerous and false. It should be hierarchically
integrated with a contextual base of experiential knowledge. Without foundations in concrete living experience, abstract knowledge becomes functionally
autonomous and divorced from the empirical foundations or the experience
it attempts to explain and organize. Such abstract knowledge may thus
dangerously live a life of its own, out of touch with reality.[47]

Maslow and Rogers' advocacy of the hierarchical integration of
phenomenological and experimental methods was meant to enlarge, not
replace, either method. Experiential knowledge is prior to conceptual knowl-

edge, but in itself it is as useless as isolated objective knowledge. Employing Buberian terminology Maslow and Rogers argued that the study of human nature should begin with "I-thou" experiential knowledge--a subjective private knowledge--and only then through ordering and systematization should this knowledge be translated into spectator "I-it" knowledge--a verifiable and more reliable level of knowledge. In Maslow's words,

> It [science] need not abdicate from the problems of love, creativeness, value, beauty, imagination, ethics and joy, leaving these altogether to "non-scientists," to poets, prophets, priests, dramatists, artists, or diplomats. All of these people may have wonderful insights, ask the questions that need to be asked, put forth challenging hypothesis, and may even be correct and true much of the time. But however sure *they* may be, they can never make mankind sure. They can convince only those who already agree with them, and a few more. Science is the only way we have of shoving truth down the reluctant throat. Only science can overcome characterological differences in seeing and believing. Only science can progress.[48]

Quantitative and phenomenological methods have their own limitations. They both fail at one time or another. None is totally safe and so they should not be used in isolation. The use of the experimental method by behaviorists is as dangerous as the exclusive use of the subjective mode by existentialists. Humanistic psychology, they advocated, is a distinct current of thought in psychology exactly because it combines both methods.

From this perspective, knowledge of human phenomena, they argued, occurs in stages or levels. Starting with simpler, tentative and exploratory boldness, the psychologist moves up to careful technical work and refinement of statement. The experimental method is definitely not the beginning, but the end of the process of knowledge acquisition. The controlled, predesigned and crucial experiment is the last or highest step in this progressive accumulation of knowledge, not the beginning. In doing so, Rogers and Maslow argued that humanistic psychologists will make the study of human nature a more inclusive science, encompassing behaviorism and existentialism.[49]

In conclusion, although Maslow and Rogers were well versed in experimental psychology, as soon as they began exploring the subjective aspects of human psychology they recognized the restrictive nature of behavioral studies and the experimental method. Their attempt to integrate positivistic psychology with their understanding of phenomenology and existentialism ostracized them from mainstream American psychology. Their ideas did not fare any better with the phenomenologists. Their suggestion to submit the phenomena of subjectivity to objective, quantitative, experimental and behavioral scrutiny was equally anathema in phenomenological and existential circles.

ENDNOTES

[1] Donald Polkinghorne, *Methodology for Human Sciences* (Albany: State University of New York Press, 1983).

[2] J. B. Watson, "Psychology as the Behaviorist Views It," *Psychological Review* 20 (1913): 158-177.

[3] E. Husserl, *Phenomenological Psychology* (trans. J. Scanlon from the German original, 1925) (The Hague: Nijhoff, 1977).

[4] A. Giorgi (Ed.), *Phenomenology and Psychological Research* (Pittsburgh: Duquesne University Press, 1984); E. Craig, "Psychotherapy for Freedom," *The Humanistic Psychologist* 16 (1988) [Special issue].

[5] T. W. Wann, *Behaviorism and Phenomenology* (Chicago: Jeremy Tarcher, 1964).

[6] R. J. DeCarvalho, *The Founders of Humanistic Psychology* (New York: Praeger, 1991); "A History of the 'Third Force' in Psychology," *Journal of Humanistic Psychology* 30 (1990): 22-44; "Carl Rogers' Naturalistic System of Ethics," *Psychological Reports* 65 (1989): 1155-1162.

[7] Rogers, "Recent Research in Nondirective Therapy and its Implications," *American Journal of Orthopsychiatry* 16 (1946): 581-588; "Research in Psychotherapy," *American Journal of Orthopsychiatry* 18 (1948): 96-100; "Training Individuals to Engage in the Therapeutic Process," in C. R. Stroher (Ed.), *Psychology and Mental Health* (Washington DC: American Psychological Association, 1957), pp. 76-92; "Psychotherapy Today," *American Journal of Psychotherapy* 17 (1963): 5-16; *Psychotherapy and Personality Change* (Chicago: University of Chicago Press, 1954), p. 13.

[8] W. U. Snyder (Ed.), *Case book of Non-Directive Counseling* (Boston: Houghton Mifflin, 1947); "Client-Centered Therapy," *The University of Chicago Round Table* 698 (1951): 12-21; *Client-Centered Therapy* (Boston: Houghton Mifflin, 1951), p. 13; *Counseling and Psychotherapy* (Boston: Houghton Mifflin, 1942); Rogers & Dymond, *Psychotherapy*, p. 27.

[9] Rogers, "The Use of Electrically Recorded Interviews in Improving Psychotherapeutic Techniques," *American Journal of Orthopsychiatry* 12 (1942): 429-434; "A Coordinated Research in Psychotherapy," *Journal Consulting Psychology* 13 (1949): 149-153; "Recent Research"; "Client-Centered Therapy," p. 12; "The Necessary and Sufficient Conditions of Therapeutic Personality Change," *Journal Consulting Psychology* 21 (1957): 95-103; *On Becoming a Person* (Boston: Houghton Mifflin, 1961), pp. 225-42.

[10] Rogers & Dymond, *Psychotherapy*, pp. 413-34; cf. Rogers, "Recent Research," p. 583.

[11] W. Stephenson, *The Study of Behavior* (Chicago: University of Chicago Press, 1953); cf. Rogers, "Person-Centered Personality Theory," in R. Corsini (Ed.), *Current Personality Theories* (Itasca: Peacock, 1977), p. 137; V. R. Raimy, *The Self-Concept as a Factor in Counseling and Personality Organization* (unpublished doctoral dissertation, Ohio State University).

[12] Rogers & Dymond, *Psychotherapy*, pp. 55,350, 429; Rogers, "Client-Centered psychotherapy," *Scientific America* 187 (1952): 66-74; "A Research Program in Client-Centered Therapy," *Research Publications Association Nervous Mental Diseases* 31 (1953): 106-113; "A Theory of Therapy Personality, and Interpersonal Relationships, as Developed in the Client-centered Framework," in S. Koch (Ed.), *Psychotherapy* (New York: McGraw-Hill, 1959), pp. 184-256.

[13] DeCarvalho, *The Founders*, chap. 4; W. Frick, *Humanistic Psychology: Interviews with Maslow, Murphy and Rogers* (Columbus: Merrill, 1971), p. 19;

Maslow, *The Psychology of Science* (New York: Harper and Row, 1966), p. 7; "Conversation with Abraham H. Maslow," *Psychology Today* 2 (1968): 34-37,54-57.

[14] Maslow, *The Effect of Varying External Conditions on Learning, Retention and Reproduction* (unpublished Master's Thesis, University of Winconsin-Madison, 1931); "The Role of Dominance in the Social and Sexual Behavior of Infra-human Primates: I, II, III," *Journal of Genetic Psychology* 48 (1936): 261-277,278-309,310-338.

[15] Maslow, "Individual Psychology and the Social Behavior of Monkeys and Apes," *International Journal of Individual Psychology* 1 (1935): 47-59.

[16] Maslow, "The Role of Dominance," p. 336; "The Comparative Approach to Social Behavior," *Social Forces* 15 (1937): 487-490.

[17] Maslow, "Self-Esteem (Dominance-Feeling) and Sexuality in Women," *Journal of Social Psychology* 16 (1942): 259-294; *Motivation and Personality* (New York: Harper, 1954), p. 61; "Effects of Esthetic Surroundings: Initial Effects of Three Esthetic Conditions Upon Perceiving 'Energy' and 'Well-being' in Faces," *Journal of Psychology* 41 (1956): 247-254; R. J. Lowry, *Dominance, Self-Esteem, Self-Actualization* (Monterey: Brooks/Cole, 1973).

[18] R. J. DeCarvalho, "Abraham H. Maslow (1908-1970): An Intellectual Biography, *Thought: Review of Culture and Idea* 66(1991).

[19] Maslow, *Motivation and Personality*, pp. 234,353-363.

[20] Maslow, *Motivation and Personality*, pp. 199-234; "Mental Health and Religion," in *Religion, Science and Mental Health* (New York: State University of New York Press, 1959), pp. 16-22; "Eupsychia-The Good Society," *Journal of Humanistic Psychology* 1 (1961): 1-11.

[21] Maslow, *Motivation and Personality*, pp. 199-234; "Personality Problems and Personality Growth," in C. Moustakas (Ed.), *The self* (New York: Harper, 1956), pp. 3-8; *Toward a Psychology of Being* (New York: Nostrand, 1962), p. 189.

[22] Maslow, *Motivation and Personality*, chap. 12.

[23] Maslow, "Some Frontier Problems in Mental Health," in A. Combs

(Ed.), *Personality Theory and Counseling Practice* (Miami: University of Florida Press, 1961), pp. 1-12; *Psychology of Being*, pp. i-v; *Motivation and Personality* (New York: Harper and Row, rev. ed. 1970), pp. x-xii; *Farther Reaches of Human Nature* (New York: Viking, 1971), p. 4; C. Wilson, *New Pathways in Psychology* (London: Gollancz, 1972).

[24] Rogers, "Autobiography," in G. Lindzey (Eds.), *History of Psychology in Autobiography* (New York: Appleton-Century-Crofts, 1967), vol. 5.

[25] Rogers, *On Becoming a Person*, p. 200; "A Personal Formulation of Client-Centered Therapy," *Marriage & Family Living* 14 (1952): 341-361.

[26] Rogers, *On Becoming a Person*, p. 163.

[27] Rogers, "Autobiography"; "Dialogue Between Martin Buber and Carl Rogers," *Psychologia* 3 (1960): 208-221.

[28] Rogers, "Toward a Science of the Person," *Journal Humanistic Psychology* 3 (1963): 72-92; *On Becoming a Person*, p. 66.

[29] Rogers, "Persons or Science: A Philosophical Question," *Cross Currents* 3 (1955): 289-306.

[30] Rogers, *On Becoming a Person*, p. 199; cf. "A Tentative Scale for the Measurement of Process in Psychotherapy," in E. A. Rubinstein and M. B. Parloff (Eds.), *Research in Psychotherapy* (Washington, DC: American Psychological Association, 1959), p. 100.

[31] Rogers, "Persons or Science?"; "A Theory of Therapy," p. 251.

[32] Rogers, "Persons or Science?"; "Some Thoughts Regarding the Current Philosophy of the Behavioral Sciences," *Journal of Humanistic Psychology* 5 (1965): 182-194.

[33] Rogers, "Persons or Science."

[34] Rogers, "Science of the Person," p. 75.

[35] Rogers, "Science of the Person," p. 77; "Persons or Science"; "Some Thoughts."

[36] Rogers, "Some Thoughts."

[37] Maslow, *The Psychology of Science; Motivation and Personality*.

[38] Maslow, "A Philosophy of Psychology," *Main Currents* 13 (1956): 27-32.

[39] Maslow, "Some Frontier Problems," p. 1.

[40] Maslow, *The Psychology of Science*, chap. 10.

[41] Maslow, *The Psychology of Science*, p. 101.

[42] Rogers, "Persons or Science?," p. 299; "Carl Rogers Speaks Out on Groups and the Lack of a Human Science," *Psychology Today* 1 (1967): 19-21,62-66; "Foreword," in A. DePeretti, *Pensee et Verite de Carl Rogers* (Toulouse: Privat, 1974), pp. 20-27; "Toward a More Human Science of the Person," *Journal Humanistic Psychology* 25 (1985): 7-24; Frick, *Humanistic Psychology*, p. 107; Rogers & Coulson, *Psychotherapy*, p. 154; Maslow, "Self-esteem," p. 260; "Some Frontier Problems"; *The Psychology of Science*, chap. 10; *Farther Reaches*, pp. 16-19.

[43] Rogers, "Science of the Person," pp. 81,90; *Dialogue Between Michael Polanyi and Carl Rogers* (San Diego: San Diego State College and Western Behavioral Sciences Institute, 1966); "Some Questions and Challenges Facing a Humanistic Psychology, *Journal Humanistic Psychology* 5 (1965): 1-5; Maslow, "Problem-Centering vs. Means-Centering in Science," *Philosophy of Science* 13 (1946): 326-331; "Comments on Dr. Frankl's Paper," *Journal of Humanistic Psychology* 6 (1966): 107-112; *The Psychology of Science*.

[44] Rogers, "Some Thoughts."

[45] Ibid., p. 187.

[46] Ibid. See also Rogers & Coulson, *Psychotherapy*, chap. 4; Maslow, "Some Frontier Problems," p. 1.

[47] Maslow, "Experimentalizing the Clinical Method," *Journal of Clinical Psychology* 1 (1945): 241-243; *Farther Reaches*, p. ix.

[48] Maslow, *Psychology of Being*, p. viii; cf. "Remarks on Existentialism and Psychology," *Existentialist Inquiries* 1 (1960): 1-5; *The Psychology of Science*, chap. 11.

[49] Rogers, *On Becoming a Person*, chap. 21; "Some Questions and Challenges." Maslow, "Comments," p. 107; *The Psychology of Science*, chap. 10; *Farther Reaches*, pp. 16-19.

Appendix 1

ABRAHAM H. MASLOW
A CHRONOLOGICAL BIBLIOGRAPHY

1932

1 Delayed reaction tests on primates from the lemur to the orangutan. (With Harry Harlow and Harold Vehling). *Journal of Comparative Psychology, 13*, 313-342.
2 Delayed reaction tests on primates at Bronx Park Zoo. (With Harry Harlow). *Journal of Comparative Psychology, 14*, 97-101.
3 The "emotion of disgust in dogs." *Journal of Comparative Psychology, 14*, 401-407.

1933

4 Food preference of primates. *Journal of Comparative Psychology, 16*, 187-197.

1934

5 Influence of differential motivation on delayed reactions in monkeys. (With Elizabeth Groshong). *Journal of Comparative Psychology, 18*, 75-83.
6 The effect of varying external conditions on learning, retention and reproduction. *Journal of Comparative Psychology, 1934, 17*, 36-47.
7 The effect of varying time intervals between acts of learning with a note on proactive inhibition. *Journal of Experimental Psychology, 17* 141-144.

1935

8 Appetites and hungers in animal motivation. *Journal of Comparative Psychology, 20*, 75-83.
9 Individual psychology and the social behavior of monkeys and apes. *Inter-*

national Journal Individual Psychology, 1, 47-59.

1936

10 The role of dominance in the social and sexual behavior of infra-human primates: I. Observations at Vilas Park Zoo. *Journal of Genetic Psychology, 48*, 261-277.

11 Part II: An experimental determination of the dominance behavior syndrome. (With Sydney Flanzbaum). *Journal of Genetic Psychology, 48*, 278-309.

12 Part III: A theory of sexual behavior of infra-human primates. *Journal of Genetic Psychology, 48*, 310-338.

13 Part IV: The determination of hierarchy in pairs and in groups. *Journal of Genetic Psychology, 49*, 161-198.

1937

14 The comparative approach to social behavior. *Social Forces, 15*, 487-490.

15 The influence of familiarization on preferences. *Journal of Experimental Psychology, 21*, 162-180.

16 Dominance-feeling, behavior and status. *Psychological Review, 44*, 404-429.

17 Personality and patterns of culture. In Ross Stagner, *Psychology of Personality*. New York: McGraw-Hill.

18 An experimental study of insight in monkeys. (With Walter Grether). *Journal of Comparative Psychology, 24*, 127-134.

1939

19 Dominance, personality and social behavior in women. *Journal of Social Psychology, 10*, 3-39.

1940

20 Dominance-quality and social behavior in infra-human primates. *Journal of Social Psychology, 11*, 313-324.

21 A test for dominance-feeling (self-esteem) in college women," *Journal of Social Psychology, 12*, 255-270.

1941

22 *Principles of abnormal psychology: The dynamic of psychic illness*. (With Bela Mittelmann). New York: Harper and Bros.

23 Deprivation, threat and frustration. *Psychological Review*, 1941, *48*, 364-366.

1942

24 Liberal leadership and personality. *Freedom, 2*, 27-30.

25 *Manual for Social Personality Inventory: A test for self-esteem in women* (with manual). Palo Alto, Calif.: Consulting Psychologists Press.
26 The dynamics of psychological security-insecurity. *Character and Personality, 10,* 331-344.
27 A comparative approach to the problem of destructiveness. *Psychiatry, 5,* 517-522.
28 Self-esteem (dominance-feeling) and sexuality in women. *Journal of Social Psychology, 16,* 259-294.

1943

29 A preface to motivation theory. *Psychosomatic Medicine, 5,* 85-92.
30 A theory of human motivation. *Psychological Review, 50,* 370-396.
31 Conflict, frustration and the theory of threat. *Journal of Abnormal and Social Psychology, 38,* 81-86.
32 The dynamics of personality organization: I & II. *Psychological Review, 50,* 514-539; 541-558. (Included in No. 57).
33 The authoritarian character structure. *Journal of Social Psychology, 18,* 401-411.

1944

34 What intelligence tests mean. *Journal of General Psychology, 31,* 85-93.

1945

35 A clinically derived test for measuring psychological security-insecurity. (With E. Birsh, M. Stein, and I. Honigman). *Journal of General Psychology, 33,* 21-41.
36 A suggested improvement in semantic usage. *Psychological Review, 52,* 239-240.
37 Experimentalizing the clinical method. *Journal of Clinical Psychology, 1,* 241-243.

1946

38 Security and breast feeding. *Journal of Abnormal and Social Psychology, 41,* 83-85. (With I. Szilagyi-Kessler).
39 Problem-centering vs. means-centering in science. *Philosophy of Science, 13,* 326-331.

1947

40 A symbol for holistic thinking. *Persona, 1,* 24-25.

1948

41 "Higher" and "lower" needs. *Journal of Psychology, 25,* 433-436. (Included

in No. 57).
42 Cognition of the particular and the generic. *Psychological Review, 55,* 22-40.
43 Some theoretical consequences of basic need-gratification. *Journal of Personality, 16,* 402-416.

1949

44 Our maligned animal nature. *Journal of Psychology, 28,* 273-278. (Included in No. 57).
45 The expressive component of behavior. *Psychological Review, 56,* 261-272. (Included in No. 57).

1950

46 Self-actualizing people: A study of psychological health. *Personality Symposia*: Symposium #1 on Values. New York: Grune and Stratton. Pp. 11-34. (Included in No. 57).

1951

47 Social theory of motivation. In M. Shore (Ed.), *Twentieth century mental hygiene.* New York: Social Science Publishers.
48 Personality. In H. Helson (Ed.), *Theoretical foundations of psychology.* New York: Van Nostrand. (With D. MacKinnon).
49 Higher needs and personality. *Dialectica* (University of Liege), *5,* 257-265. (Included in No. 57).
50 Resistance to acculturation. *Journal of Social Issues, 7,* 26-29. (Included in No. 57).
51 *Principles of abnormal psychology* (Rev. Ed.) Harper & Bros. (With B. Mittelman).

1952

52 Volunteer-error in the Kinsey study. (With J. Sakoda). *Journal of Abnormal and Social Psychology, 47,* 259-262.
53 The S-I Test (A measure of psychological security and insecurity). Consulting Psychologists Press, Palo Alto, California.

1953

54 Love in healthy people. In A. Montagu (Ed.), *The meaning of love.* New York: Julian Press. Pp. 57-93. (Included in No. 57).
55 College teaching ability, scholarly activity and personality. *Journal of Educational Psychology, 47,* 185-189.

1954

56 The instinctoid nature of basic needs. *Journal of Personality, 22*, 326-347.
57 Motivation and personality. New York: Harper & Bros. (Includes papers 23,27,29,30,31,32,39,41,42,43,44,45,46,49,50, 54,56,59).
58 "Abnormal psychology"-*National Encyclopedia.*
59 Normality, health and values. *Main Currents, 10*, 75-81. (Included in No. 57).

1955

60 Deficiency motivation and growth motivation. In M. R. Jones (Ed.), *Nebraska symposium in motivation: 1955*, Lincoln, Nebr.: University. of Nebraska Press. (Included in No. 87).
60a Comments on Prof. McClelland's paper. In M. R. Jones (Ed.), *Nebraska symposium on motivation, 1955*. Lincoln, Nebr.: University of Nebraska Press. Pp. 65-142.
60b Comments on Prof. Old's paper. In M. R. Jones, (Ed.), *Nebraska symposium in motivation, 1955*. Lincoln, Nebr.: University of Nebraska Press. Pp. 143-147.

1956

61 Effects of esthetic surroundings: I. Initial effects of three esthetic conditions upon perceiving 'energy' and 'well-being' in faces. (With N. L. Mintz). *Journal of Psychology, 41*, 247-254.
62 Personality problems and personality growth. In C. Moustakas (Ed.), *The self*. New York: Harper.
63 Defense and growth. *Merrill-Palmer Quarterly, 3*, 36-47. (Included in No. 87).
64 A philosophy of psychology. *Main Currents, 13*, 27-32.

1957

65 Power relationships and patterns of personal development. In A. Kornhauser (Ed.), *Problems of power in American democracy*. Detroit: Wayne University Press.
66 Security of judges as a factor in impressions of warmth in others. (With J. Bossom). *Journal of Abnormal and Social Psychology, 55*, 147-148.
67 Two kinds of cognition and their integration. *General Semantics Bulletin, 20 & 21*, 17-22.

1958

68 Emotional blocks to creativity. *Journal of Individual Psychology, 14*, 51-56.

1959

69 Psychological data and human values. In A. H. Maslow (Ed.), *New knowledge in human values*. New York: Harpers. (Included in No. 87).

70 Editor, *New knowledge in human values*. New York: Harpers.
71 Creativity in self-actualizing people. In H. H. Anderson, (Ed.), *Creativity and its cultivation*. New York: Harper. (Included in No. 87).
72 Cognition of being in the peak experiences. *Journal of Genetic Psychology, 94*, 43-66.
73 Mental health and religion. In *Religion, science and mental health*. Academy of Religion and Mental Health, New York University Press.
74 Critique of self-actualization; I: Some dangers of Being-cognition. *Journal of Individual Psychology, 15*, 24-32.

1960

75 Juvenile delinquency as a value disturbance. (With R. Diaz-Guerrero). In J. Peatman and E. Hartley (Eds.), *Festschrift for Gardner Murphy*. New York: Harper.
76 Remarks on existentialism and psychology. *Existentialist Inquiries, 1*, 1-5. (Included in No. 87).
77 Resistance to being rubricized. In B. Kaplan and S. Wapner, (Eds.), *Perspective in psychological theory, essays in honor of Heinz Werner*. International Universities Press. (Included in No. 87).
78 Some parallels between the dominance and sexual behavior of monkeys and the fantasies of patients in psychotherapy. (With H. Rand & S. Newman). *Journal of Nervous and Mental Disease, 131*, 202-212.

1961

79 Health as transcendence of the environment. *Journal of Humanistic Psychology, 1*, 1-7. (Included in No. 87).
80 Peak experiences as acute identity experiences. *American Journal of Psychoanalysis 21*, 254-260. (Included in No. 87).
81 Eupsychia-The good society. *Journal of Humanistic Psychology, 1*, 1-11.
82 Are our publications and conventions suitable for the personal psychologies? *American Psychologist, 16* 318-319. (included in No. 87).
83 Comments on Skinner's attitude to science. *Daedalus, 90*, 572-573.
84 Some frontier problems in mental health. In A. Combs (Ed.), *Personality theory and counseling practice*. University of Florida Press.
85 Summary Comments: Symposium on Human Values. In L. Solomon (Ed.), *WBSI Report* No. *17*, 1961, 41-44.

1962

86 Some basic propositions of a growth and self-actualization psychology. In A. Combs (Ed.), *Perceiving, behaving, becoming: A new ,focus for education. 1962 Yearbook of Association for Supervision and Curriculum Development*. Washington, D.C. (Included in No. 87).
87 *Toward a psychology of being*. Princeton, N.J.: Nostrand. (Includes papers 60,62,63,69,71,72,74, 76,77,79,80,82,86,93).
88 Book review: John Schaar, Escape from Authority. *Humanist, 22*, 34-35.

89 Lessons from the peak-experiences. *Journal of Humanistic Psychology, 2,* 9-18.
90 Notes on Being-Psychology. *Journal of Humanistic Psychology, 2,* 47-71.
91 Was Adler a disciple of Freud? A note. *Journal of Individual Psychology, 18,* 125.
92 Summer notes on social psychology of industry and management. Delmar, California: Non-Linear Systems, Inc., 1962. (Includes papers Nos. 97,100,101,104). Edited and improved revision published as *Eupsychian management: A journal.* Irwin-Dorsey, 1965.

1963

93 The need to know and the fear of knowing. *Journal of General Psychology, 68,* 111-125. (Included in No. 87).
94 The creative attitude. *The Structurist,* No. *3,* 4-10.
95 Fusion of facts and values. *American Journal of Psychoanalysis, 23,* 117-131.
96 Criteria for judging needs to be instinctoid. *Proceedings of 1963 International Congress of Psychology.* Amsterdam: North-Holland Publishers, 1964. Pp. 86-87.
97 Further notes on Being-Psychology. *Journal of Humanistic Psychology, 3,* 120-135.
98 Notes on innocent cognition. In L. Schenk-Danzinger & H. Thomas (Eds.), *Gegenwartsprobleme der Entwicklungs psychologie: Festschrift fur Charlotte Buhler,* Gottingen: Verlag fur psychologie, 1963.
99 The scientific study of values. *Proceedings 7th Congress of Inter-American Society of Psychology.* Mexico, D.F., 1963.
100 Notes on unstructured groups. *Human Relations Training News, 7,* 1-4. (Included in No. 112).

1964

101 The superior person. *Trans-Action, 1,* 10-13. (Included in No. 112).
102 *Religion, values and peak-experiences.* Columbus, Ohio: Ohio State University Press.
103 Synergy in the society and in the individual. (With L. Gross.) *Journal of Individual Psychology, 20,* 153-164.
104 Further notes on the Psychology of Being. *Journal of Humanistic Psychology, 4,* 45-58.
105 Preface to Japanese translation of *Toward a psychology of being.* Tokyo: Seishin-Shobo.

1965

106 Observing and reporting education experiments. *Humanist, 25,* 13.
107 Foreword to Andras Angyal, *Neurosis and treatment: A holistic theory.* Wiley. Pp. v-vii.
108 The need for creative people. *Personnel Administration, 28,* 3-5,21-22.

109 Critique and discussion. In J. Money (Ed.), *Sex research: New developments*. Holt, Rinehart and Winston. Pp. 135-143,144-146.
110 Humanistic science and transcendent experiences. *Journal of Humanistic Psychology, 5*, 219-227.
111 Criteria for judging needs to be instinctoid. In M. R. Jones (Ed.), *Human motivation: A symposium*. Lincoln, Nebr.: University of Nebraska Press. Pp. 33-47.
112 *Eupsychian management: A journal*. Homewood, Ill.: Irwin-Dorsey. (Edited version of No. 92).(Includes papers No. 100,101).
113 Art judgment and the judgment of others: A preliminary study. (With R. Morant). *Journal Clinical Psychology, 21*, 389-391.

1966

114 Isomorphic interrelationships between knower and known. In G. Kepes (Ed.), *Sign, image, symbol*. New York: Braziller.
115 *The psychology of science: A reconnaissance*. New York: Harper and Row. (Includes paper No. 110). Paperback edition, Regnery, 1969.
116 Toward a psychology of religious awareness. *Explorations, 9*, 23-41.
117 Comments on Dr. Frankl's paper. *Journal of Humanistic Psychology, 6*, 107-112.

1967

118 Neurosis as a failure of personal growth. *Humanitas, 3*, 153-169.
119 Synanon and Eupsychia. *Journal of Humanistic Psychology, 7*, 28-35.
120 Preface to Japanese translation of *Eupsychian management*. (Included in No. 128).
121 A theory of metamotivation: The biological rooting of the value-life. *Journal of Humanistic Psychology, 7*, 93-127.
122 Dialogue on communication. (With E. M. Drews). In A. Hitchcock (Ed.), *Guidance and the utilization of new educational Media: Report of the 1962 Conference*. Washington, D.C.: American Personnel and Guidance Association. Pp. 1-47,63-68.
123 Foreword to Japanese translation of *Motivation and personality*.
124 Self-actualizing and beyond. In J. F. T. Bugental (Ed.), *Challenges of humanistic psychology*. New York: McGraw-Hill.

1968

125 Music, education and peak-experiences. *Music Educators Journal, 54*, 72-75,163-171.
126 Human potentialities and the healthy society. In Herbert Otto (Ed.), *Human potentialities*. St. Louis, Missouri: Warren H. Green, Inc.
127 The new science of man. In papers on *"The human potential"*. New York: Twentieth Century Fund.
128 *Toward a psychology of being* (2nd Ed.). Princeton, N.J.: Van Nostrand.
129 Conversation with Abraham H. Maslow. *Psychology Today, 2*, 34-37,54-

57.
130 Toward the study of violence. In L. Ng Larry, (Ed.), *Alternatives to violence*. New York: Time-Life Books.
131 Some educational implications of the humanistic psychologies. *Harvard Educational Review, 38,* 685-696.
132 Goals of humanistic education. *Esalen Papers,* Big Sur, Calif.: Esalen Institute. Pp 1-24.
133 Maslow and Self-actualization (Film). Santa Ana, Calif.: Psychological Films. Santa Ana, California.
134 Some fundamental questions that face the normative social psychologist. *Journal of Humanistic Psychology, 8,* 143-154.
134a Eupsychian Network. Mimeographed. (Included in No. 128).

1969

135 The farther reaches of human nature. *Journal of Transpersonal Psychology, 1,* 1-9.
135a Theory Z. *Journal of Transpersonal Psychology, 1,* 31-47.
136 Various meanings of transcendence. *Journal of Transpersonal Psychology, 1,* 56-66.
137 A holistic approach to creativity. In C. W. Taylor (Ed.), *A climate for creativity: Reports of the Seventh National Research Conference on Creativity, University of Utah, Dec., 1968.* Salt Lake City, Utah.
138 *The healthy personality: Readings.* (With Hung-Min Chiang), New York: Nostrand, Reinhold.
139 Notice biographique et bibliographique. *Revue de Psychologie Applique, 18,* 167-173.
140 Toward a humanistic biology. *American Psychologist, 24,* 724-725.
141 Humanistic education vs. professional education. *New Directions in Teaching, 2,* 6-8.

1970

142 *Motivation and personality* (Rev. Ed.). New York: Harper and Row.
143 Humanistic education vs. professional education. *New Directions in Teaching, 2,* 3-10.
144 Abraham H. Maslow: A bibliography. *Journal of Humanistic Psychology, 10,* 98-110.

1971

145 *Farther reaches of human nature.* New York: Viking.
146 *Humanistic psychology: Interview with Maslow, Murphy and Rogers.* By W. B. Frick. Columbus, Ohio: Merrill. Pp. 19-49.

1972

147 International Study Project. *Abraham H. Maslow: A memorial volume.*

Monterey, Calif.: Brooks/Cole.

1973

148 *Dominance, self-esteem, self-actualization: Germinal papers of A. H. Maslow.* R. J. Lowry (Ed.). Monterey, Calif.: Brooks/Cole.

1979

149 *The journals of A. H. Maslow, Vol I & II.* R. J. Lowry (Ed.), Monterey, Calif.: Brooks/Cole.

Works About Maslow

Daniels, Michael. The development of the concept of self-actualization in the writings of Abraham Maslow. *Current Psychological Review* 2 (1982): 61-75.

Dennis, Lawrence. Maslow and education. *Educational Forum* 40 (1975): 49-54.

Farmer, Rodney. Maslow and values education. *Social Studies* 69 (1978): 69-73.

Goble, Frank. *The third force: The psychology of Abraham H. Maslow* (New York: Grossman Publishers, 1970).

Hoffman, Edward. *The right to be human: A biography of Abraham Maslow* (Los Angeles: Jeremy P. Tarcher, 1988).

Lowry, Richard. *A. H. Maslow: An intellectual portrait* (Monterey: Brooks/Cole, 1973).

Maddi, S. R. & Costa, P. I. *Humanism in personology: Allport. Maslow and Murray* (Chicago: Aldine/Atherton, 1972).

Roberts, Thomas B. *Maslow's human motivation needs hierarchy: A bibliography* (Research in Education, 1973, ED-069-591).

Scheele, Jenny. *Register referring to the complete published works by A. H. Maslow* (Delft, The Netherlands: Delft University of Technology, 1978).

Wilson, Colin. *New pathways in psychology: Maslow and the post-Freudian revolution* (New York: New American Library, 1972).

Appendix 2

CARL R. ROGERS
A CHRONOLOGICAL BIBLIOGRAPHY

1930

With C. W. Carson. Intelligence as a factor in camping activities. *Camping Magazine*, 1930, *3*(3):8-11.

1931

Measuring personality adjustment in children nine to thirteen. New York: Teachers College, Columbia University, Bureau of Publications, 1931.
A test of personality adjustment. New York: Association Press, 1931.
With M. E. Rappaport. We pay for the Smiths. *Survey Graphic*, 1931, *19*, 508 ff.

1933

A good foster home: Its achievements and limitations. *Mental Hygiene*, 1933, *17*, 21-40.

1936

Social workers and legislation. *Quarterly Bulletin New York State Conference on Social Work*, 1936, 7(3):3-9.

1937

The clinical psychologist's approach to personality problems. *The Family*, 1937, *18*, 233-243.
Three surveys of treatment measures used with children. *Amer. J. Orthopsychiat.*, 1937, 7, 48-57.

1938

A diagnostic study of Rochester youth. *N.Y. State Conference on Social Work.* Syracuse: 1938, pp. 48-54.

1939

Authority and case work-Are they compatible? *Quarterly Bulletin, N.Y. State Conference on Social Work.* Albany: 1939, pp. 16-24.
The Clinical Treatment of the Problem Child. Boston: Houghton Mifflin, 1939.
Needed emphases in the training of clinical psychologists. *J. Consult. Psychol.,* 1939, *3*, 141-143.

1940

The processes of therapy. *J. Consult. Psychol.,* 1940, *4*, 161-164.

1941

Psychology in clinical practice. In J. S. Gray (Ed.), *Psychology in use.* New York: American Book Company, 1941, pp. 114-167.
With C. C. Bennett. The clinical significance of problem syndromes. *Amer. J. Orthopsychiat.,* 1941, *11*, 210-221.

1942

Counseling and psychotherapy. Boston: Houghton Mifflin, 1942.
Mental health findings in three elementary schools. *Educ. Research Bulletin,* 1942, *21*, 69-79.
The psychologist's contributions to parent, child, and community problems. *J. Consult. Psychol.,* 1942, *6*, 8-18.
A study of the mental health problems in three representative elementary schools. In T. C. Holy et. al., *A study of health and physical education in Columbus public schools.* Ohio State Univer., Bur. of Educ. Res. Monogr., No. 25, 1942, pp. 130-161.
The use of electrically recorded interviews in improving psychotherapeutic techniques. *Amer. J. Orthopsychiat.,* 1942, *12*, 429-434.

1943

Therapy in guidance clinics. *J. Abnorm. Soc. Psychol.,* 1943, *38*, 284-289.

1944

Adjustment after combat. Army Air Forces Flexible Gunnery School, Fort Myers, Florida. Restricted Publication, 1944.
The development of insight in a counseling relationship. *J. Consult. Psychol.,* 1944, *8*, 331-341.

The psychological adjustments of discharged service personnel. *Psych. Bulletin*, 1944, *41*, 689-696.

1945

Counseling. *Review of Educ. Research*, 1945, *15*, 155-163.
A counseling viewpoint for the USO worker. *USO Program Services Bulletin*, 1945.
Dealing with individuals in USO. *USO Program Services Bulletin*, 1945.
The nondirective method as a technique for social research. *Amer. J. Sociology*, 1945, *50*, 279-283.
With V. M. Axline. A teacher-therapist deals with a handicapped child. *J. Abnorm. Soc. Psychol.*, 1945, *40*, 119-142.
With R. Dicks & S. B. Wortis. Current trends in counseling, a symposium. *Marriage & Family Living* 1945, 7(4).

1946

Psychometric tests and client-centered counseling. *Educ. Psychol. Measmt.*, 1946, *6*, 139-144.
Recent research in nondirective therapy and its implications. *Amer. J. Orthopsychiat.*, 1946, *16*, 581-588.
Significant aspects of client-centered therapy. *Amer. Psychologist*, 1946, *1*, 415-422.
With G. A. Muench. Counseling of emotional blocking in an aviator. *J. Abnorm. Soc. Psychol.*, 1946, *41*, 207-216.
With J. L. Wallen. Counseling with returned servicemen. New York: McGraw-Hill, 1946.

1947

The case of Mary Jane Tilden. In W. U. Snyder (Ed.), *Casebook of nondirective counseling.* Boston: Houghton Mifflin, 1947, pp. 129-203.
Current trends in psychotherapy. In W. Dennis (Ed.), *Current trends in psychology*, University of Pittsburgh Press, 1947, pp. 109-137.
Some observations on the organization of personality. *Amer. Psychologist*, 1947, *2*, 358-368.

1948

Dealing with social tensions: A presentation of client-centered counseling as a means of handling interpersonal conflict. New York: Hinds, Hayden and Eldredge, Inc., 1948.
Divergent trends in methods of improving adjustment. *Harvard Educational Review*, 1948, *18*, 209-219.
Research in psychotherapy: Round table, 1947. *Amer. J. Orthopsychiat.*, 1948, *18*, 96-100.
Some implications of client-centered counseling for college personnel work.

Educ. Psychol Measmt., 1948, *8*, 540-549.
With B. Kell & H. McNeil. The role of self-understanding in the prediction of behavior. *J. Consult. Psychol.*, 1948, *12*, 174-186.

1949

The attitude and orientation of the counselor in client-centered therapy. *J. Consult. Psychol.*, 1949, *13*, 82-94.
A coordinated research in psychotherapy: A non-objective introduction. *J. Consult. Psychol.*, 1949, *13*, 149-153.

1950

A current formulation of client-centered therapy. *Social Services Review*, 1950, *24*, 442-450.
The significance of the self-regarding attitudes and perceptions. In M. L. Reymert (Ed.), *Feelings & emotions*, New York: McGraw-Hill, 1950, pp. 374-382.
What is to be our basic professional relationship? *Annals of Allergy*, 1950, *8*, 234-239.
With R. Becker. A basic orientation for counseling. *Pastoral Psychology*, 1950, *1*(1), 26-34.
With D. G. Marquis & E. R. Hilgard. ABEPP policies and procedures. *Amer. Psychologist*, 1950, *5*, 407-408.

1951

Client-centered therapy: A helping process. *The University of Chicago Round Table*, 1951, *698*, 12-21.
Client-centered therapy: Its current practice, implications, and theory. Boston: Houghton Mifflin, 1951.
Perceptual reorganization in client-centered therapy. In R. R. Blake & G. V. Ramsey (Eds.), *Perceptions: An approach to personality.* New York: Ronald Press, 1951, pp. 307-327.
Studies in client-centered psychotherapy III: The case of Mrs. Oak--A research analysis. *Psychol. Serv. Center J.*, 1951, *3*, 47-165.
Through the eyes of a client. *Pastoral Psychology*, 1951, *2*(16), 32-40; (17):45-50.
Where are we going in clinical psychology? *J. Consult. Psychol.*, 1951, *15*, 171-177.
With T. Gordon, D. L. Grummon, & J. Seeman. Studies in client-centered psychotherapy I: Developing a program of research in psychotherapy. *Psychol. Serv. Center J.*, 1951, *3*, 3-28.

1952

Client-centered psychotherapy. *Scientific American*, 1952, *187*, 66-74.
Communication: Its blocking & facilitation. *Northwestern University Informa-*

tion, 1952, *20*, 9-15.
A personal formulation of client-centered therapy. *Marriage & Family Living*, 1952, *14*, 341-361.
With R. H. Segel. *Client-centered therapy*. 16mm. motion picture with sound. State College, Pa.: Psychological Cinema Register, 1952.
With F. J. Roethlisberger. Barriers and gateways to communication. *Harvard Business Rev.*, July-Aug. 1952, pp. 28-34.

1953

The interest in the practice of psychotherapy. *Amer. Psychologist*, 1953, *8*, 48-50.
A research program in client-centered therapy. *Res. Publ. Ass. Nerv. Ment. Dis.*, 1953, *31*, 106-113.
Some directions and end points in therapy. In O. H. Mowrer (Ed.), *Psychotherapy: Theory & research*, New York: Ronald Press, 1953, pp. 44-68.
With G. W. Brooks, R. S. Driver, W. V. Merrihue, P. Pigors, & A. J. Rinella. Removing the obstacles to good employee communications. *Management Record*, 1953, *15*(1), 9-11.
Counseling as I see it. Transcript of a talk at the Guidance and Counseling Department of San Francisco State College in 1953.

1954

Becoming a person. Oberlin College Nellie Heldt Lecture Series, Oberlin: Oberlin Printing Co., 1954.
The case of Mr. Bebb: The analysis of a failure case. In C. R. Rogers & R. F. Dymond (Eds.), *Psychotherapy and personality*. University of Chicago Press, 1954, pp. 349-409.
Changes in the maturity of behavior as related to therapy. In C. R. Rogers & R. F. Dymond (Eds.), *Psychotherapy and personality*. University of Chicago Press, 1954, pp. 215-237.
An overview of the research and some questions for the future. In C. R. Rogers & R. F. Dymond (Eds.), *Psychotherapy and personality*. University of Chicago Press, 1954, pp. 413-434.
Towards a theory of creativity. *ETC: A Review of General Semantics*, 1954, *11*, 249-260.
With R. F. Dymond (Eds.). Psychotherapy & personality change. Chicago: University of Chicago Press.

1955

A personal view of some issues facing psychologists. *Amer. Psychologist*, 1955, *10*, 247-249.
Personality change in psychotherapy. *The International J. of Social Psychiatry*, 1955, *1*, 31-41.
Persons or science? A philosophical question. *Amer. Psychologist*, 1955, *10*, 267-278.

With R. H. Siegel. *Psychotherapy begins: The case of Mr. Lin, 16 mm. motion picture with sound.* State College, Pa.: Psychological Cinema Register, 1955.
With R. H. Siegel. *Psychotherapy in process: The case of Miss Mun, 16 mm. motion picture with sound.* State College, Pa.: Psychological Cinema Register, 1955.

1956

Client-centered therapy: A current view. In F. Fromm-Reichmann & J. L. Moreno (Eds.), *Progress in psychotherapy.* New York: Grune & Stratton, 1956, pp. 199-209.
A counseling approach to human problems. *Amer. J. of Nursing,* 1956, *56,* 994-997.
Implications of recent advances in the prediction and control of behavior. *Teachers College Record,* 1956, *57,* 316-322.
Intellectualized psychotherapy. Review of George Kelly's *The psychology of personal constructs, Contemporary Psychology,* 1956, *1,* 357-358.
Review of Reinhold Niebuhr's *The self and the dramas of history, Chicago Theological Seminary Register,* 1956, *46,* 13-14.
Some issues concerning the control of human behavior. (Symposium with B. F. Skinner) *Science,* November 1956, *124,* No. 3231, 1057-1066.
What it means to become a person. In C. E. Moustakas (Ed.), *The self.* New York: Harper and Bros., 1956, pp. 195-211.
With E. J. Shoben, O. H. Mowrer, G. A. Kimble, & J. G. Miller. Behavior theories and a counseling case. *J. Counseling Psychol.,* 1956, *3,* 107-124.

1957

The necessary and sufficient conditions of therapeutic personality change. *J. Consult. Psychol.,* 1957, *21,* 95-103.
A note on the nature of man. *J. Counseling Psychol.,* 1957, *4,* 199-203.
Personal thoughts on teaching and learning. *Merrill-Palmer Quarterly,* 1957, *3,* 241-243.
A therapist view of the good life. *The Humanist,* 1957, *17,* 291-300.
Training individuals to engage in the therapeutic process. In C. R. Strother (Ed.), *Psychology and mental health.* Washington, D.C.: American Psychological Association, 1957, pp. 76-92.
With R. E. Farson. *Active listening.* University of Chicago, Industrial Relations Center, 1957.

1958

The characteristics of a helping relationship. *Personnel & Guidance Journal,* 1958, *37,* 6-16.
A process conception of psychotherapy. *American Psychologist,* 1958, *13,* 142-149.

Listening and understanding. *The Friend*, 1958, *116*(40), 1248-1251.

1959

Client-centered therapy. In S. Arieti (Ed.), *American Handbook of Psychiatry*, Vol. 3. New York: Basic Books, Inc., 1959, pp. 183-200.

Comments on cases in S. Standal & R. Corsini (Eds.), *Critical incidents in psychotherapy*. New York: Prentice-Hall, 1959.

The essence of psychotherapy: A client-centered view. *Annals of Psychotherapy*, 1959, *1*, 51-57.

Lessons I have learned in counseling with individuals. In W. E. Dugan (Ed.), *Modern school practices, Series 3, Counseling points of view*. University of Minnesota Press, 1959, pp. 14-26.

Significant learning: In therapy and in education. *Educational Leadership*, 1959, *16*, 232-242.

A tentative scale for the measurement of process in psychotherapy. In E. A. Rubinstein & M. B. Parloff (Eds.), *Research in psychotherapy*. Washington, D.C.: American Psychological Association, 1959, pp. 96-107.

A theory of therapy, personality, and interpersonal relationships, as developed in the client-centered framework. In S. Koch (Ed.), *Psychology: A study of a science*. New York: McGraw-Hill, 1959, pp. 184-256.

The way is to be. Review of Rollo May, et. al., *Existence: A new dimension in psychiatry and psychology*. *Contemporary Psychology*, 1959, *4*, 196-198.

With G. Marian Kinget. *Psychotherapie en Menselyke Verhoudingen*. Utrecht: Uitgeverij Het Spectrum, 1959.

With M. Lewis & J. J. Shlien. Time-limited, client-centered psychotherapy: Two cases. In A. Burton (Ed.), *Case studies of counseling and psychotherapy*. Prentice-Hall, 1959, pp. 309-352.

Counseling theory and techniques: A panel discussion. In W. E. Dugan (Ed.), *Modern school practices, Series 3, Counseling points of view*. University of Minnesota Press, 1959, pp. 27-47.

1960

Dialogue between Martin Buber and Carl Rogers. *Psychologia*, 1960, *3*(4), 208-221.

Psychotherapy: The counselor, and psychotherapy: The client, 16 mm. motion pictures with sound. Bureau of Audio Visual Aids, University of Winconsin, 1960.

Significant trends in the client-centered orientation. In D. Brower & L. E. Abt (Eds.), *Progress in clinical psychology*, Vol. IV. New York: Grune & Stratton, 1960, pp. 85-99.

A therapist's view of personal goals. *Pendle Hill Pamphlet, No. 108*. Wallingford, Pennsylvania, 1960.

With A. Walker & R. Rablen. Development of a scale to measure process change in psychotherapy. *J. Clinical Psychol.*, 1960, *16*(1), 79-85.

1961

The loneliness of contemporary man as seen in "The Case of Ellen West", *Review of Existential Psychology & Psychiatry*, 1961, *1*(2), 94-101.

Panel presentation: The client-centered approach to certain questions regarding psychotherapy. *Annals of Psychotherapy*, 1961, *2*, 51-53.

The place of the person in the new world of the behavioral sciences. *Personnel & Guidance Journal*, 1961, *39*(6), 442-451.

The process equation of psychotherapy. *American Journal of Psychotherapy*, 1961, *15*(1), 27-45.

A theory of psychotherapy with schizophrenics and a proposal for its empirical investigation. In J. G. Dawson, H. K. Stone & N. P. Dellis (Eds.), *Psychotherapy with schizophrenics*, Baton Rouge: Louisiana State University Press, 1961, pp. 3-19.

Two divergent trends. In R. May (Ed.), *Existential psychology*. New York: Random House, 1961, pp. 85-93.

What we know about psychotherapy. *Pastoral Psychology*, 1961, *12*, 31-38.

Personality adjustment inventory. New York: Association Press, 1961. (Slightly revised form of the 1931 edition.)

The significance or meaning of the study to date. *The Psychiatric Institute Bull.* (University of Wisconsin-Madison), 1961, *1*(10), 1-5.

Introduction to the symposium. *The Psychiatric Institute Bull.*, 1961, *1*(10a), 1-5.

The developing values of the growing person. *The Psychiatric Institute Bull.*, 1961, *1*(13), 1-15.

Comments on cultural evolution as viewed by psychologists. *Daedalus*, 1961, *90*, 574-575.

1962

Comment (on article by F. L. Vance). *J. Counsel. Psychol.*, 1962, *9*, 16-17.

The interpersonal relationship: The core of guidance. *Harvard Educ. Rev.*, 1962, *32*(4), 416-429.

Niebuhr on the nature of man. In S. Doniger (Ed.), *The nature of man.* New York: Harper and Brothers, 1962, pp. 55-71 (with discussion by B. M. Loomer, W. M. Horton, & H. Hofmann).

Some learnings from a study of psychotherapy with schizophrenics. *Pennsylvania Psychiatric Quarterly*, Summer 1962, pp. 3-15.

A study of psychotherapeutic change in schizophrenic and normals: Design and instrumentation. *Psychiatric Research Reports*, American Psychiatric Association, 1962, *15*, 51-60.

The therapeutic relationship: Recent theory & research. Lecture given under sponsorship of the Los Angeles Society of Clinical Psychologists in Beverly Hills, California, January 19, 1962. Privately printed.

Toward becoming a fully functioning person. In A. W. Combs (Ed.), *Perceiving, behaving, becoming, 1962 Yearbook.* Association for Supervision and Curriculum Development. Washington, D.C., 1962, pp. 21-31.

With G. M. Kinget. *Psychotherapie et relations humaines: Theorie et pratique*

de la therapie non-directive. Louvain, Belgium: Publications Universitaires, 1962.
Enseigner et apprendre. *Education Nationale,* 1962, *22,* 12-14.

1963

The actualizing tendency in relation to "motives" and to consciousness. In M. Jones (Ed.), *Nebraska Symposium on Motivation, 1963.* University of Nebraska, 1963, pp. 1-24.
The concept of the fully functioning person. *Psychotherapy: Theory, Research, and Practice,* 1963, *1*(1), 17-26.
Learning to be free. In S. M. Farber & R. H. Wilson (Eds.), *Conflict and creativity: Control of the mind, Part 2.* New York: McGraw-Hill, 1963, pp. 268-288.
Learning to be free. (Condensation of above) *Nat. Educ. Ass. J.,* March 1963.
Psychotherapy today: Or, where do we go from here? *American Journal of Psychotherapy,* 1963, *17*(1), 5-16.
La relation therapeutic: Les bases de son efficacite. *Bulletin de Psychologie,* 1963, *17*(1), 1-9.
Towards a science of the person. *J. Hum. Psychol.,* 1963, *3*(2), :72-92.

1964

Freedom and commitment. *The Humanist,* 1964, *24*(2), 37-40.
Some elements of effective interpersonal communication. Lecture at California Institute of Technology, November 1964. Unpublished.
Toward a modern approach to values: The valuing process in the mature person. *J. Abnorm. Soc. Psy.,* 1964, *68*(2), 160-167.
Toward a science of the person. In T. W. Wann (Ed.), *Behaviorism and phenomenology: Contrasting bases for modern psychology.* University of Chicago Press, 1964, pp. 109-140.
What psychology has to offer to teacher education. La Jolla, California: WBSI, 1964.
Some elements of effective interpersonal communication. La Jolla, California: WBSI, 1964.

1965

An afternoon with Carl Rogers. *Explorations,* 1965, *3,* 1-4.
Can we meet the need for counseling? A suggested plan. *Marriage & Family,* 1965, *2*(5), 4-6. Queensland, Australia: National Marriage Guidance Council of Australia.
Dealing with psychological tensions. *J. Appl. Behav. Sci.,* 1965, *1,* 6-24.
Foreword. In H. Anderson, *Creativity in Childhood and Adolescence.* Palo Alto: Science and Behavior Books, 1965, pp. v-vii.
A humanistic conception of man. In R. E. Farson (Ed.), *Science and human affairs.* Palo Alto California: Science and Behavior Books, 1965, pp. 18-31.

Psychology and teacher training. In D. B. Gowan & C. Richardson (Eds.),
   Five fields and teacher training. Ithaca, New York: Project One Publi-
   cation, Cornell University, 1965, pp. 56-91.
Some questions and challenges facing a humanistic psychology. *J. Hum.
   Psychol*, 1965, *5*, 1-5.
The therapeutic relationship: Recent theory and research. *Australian Journal
   of Psychology*, 1965, *17*, 95-108.
A wife's-eye view of Carl Rogers. *Voices*, 1965, *1*(1), 93-98. By Helen E.
   Rogers.
The potential of the human individual: The capacity for becoming fully func-
   tioning. *Journal of Education*, 1965, *22*, 1-14.
Some thoughts regarding the current philosophy of the behavioral sciences. *J.
   Hum. Psychol*, 1965, *5*(2), 182-194.
The basic encounter group and its process. Transcript of a lecture delivered at
   the Atlanta Psychiatric Clinic, September, 1965.
Interview. In C. A. Dallis, *The development of Rogerian thought and its impli-
   cations for counselor education*. Unpublished doctoral dissertation,
   University of Winconsin-Madison, 1965.

1966

Client-centered therapy. In S. Arieti (Ed.), *Supplement to American Hand-
   book of Psychiatry*, Vol. 3. New York: Basic Books, Inc., 1966, pp. 185-
   200. (See also 1959).
Dialogue between Michael Polanyi and Carl Rogers. San Diego: San Diego
   State College and Western Behavioral Sciences Institute, July 1966.
Dialogue between Paul Tillich and Carl Rogers, Parts I & II. San Diego: San
   Diego State College, 1966.
To facilitate learning. In M. Provus (Ed.), *Innovations for time to teach*.
   Washington, D.C.: National Education Association, 1966, pp. 4-19.

1967

Autobiography. In E. W. Boring & G. Lindzey, *A history of psychology in
   autobiography*, Vol. 5. New York: Appleton-Century-Crofts, 1967.
Carl Rogers speaks out on group and the lack of a human science. An interview. Psychology Today, December 1967, *1*, 19-21,62-66.
Client-centered therapy. In A. M. Freedman & H. I. Kaplan (Eds.), *Comprehensive textbook of psychiatry*. Baltimore: Williams & Wilkins, 1967,
   pp. 1225-1228.
The facilitation of significant learning. In L. Siegel (Ed.), *Contemporary theories of instruction*. San Francisco: Chandler Publishing Co., 1967, pp.
   37-54.
The interpersonal relationship in the facilitation of learning. In R. Leeper
   (Ed.), *Humanizing education*. National Education Association, Association for Supervision and Curriculum Development, 1967.
A plan for self-directed change in an educational system. *Educ. Leadership*,
   1967, *24*, 717-731.

The process of the basic encounter group. In J. F. T. Bugental (Ed.), *Challenges of humanistic psychology*. New York: McGraw-Hill, 1967, pp. 261-278.
With E. T. Gendlin, D. J. Kiesler, & C. Truax. *The Therapeutic relationship and its impact: A study of psychotherapy with schizophrenic*. University of Wisconsin Press, 1967.
With B. Stevens et al. *Person to Person*. Moab, Utah: Real People Press, 1967.
With E. M. Drews & A. H. Maslow. Panel discussion. In A. A. Hitchcock (Ed.), Guidance and the utilization of new educational media: Report of the 1962 Conference, Washington, D.C.: American Personnel & Guidance Association, 1967, pp. 49-78.

1968

The interpersonal relationship in the facilitation of learning. *The Virgil E. Herrick Memorial Lecture Series*. Columbus, Ohio: Charles E. Merrill Publishing Co., 1968.
Interpersonal relationships: USA 2000. *J. Appl. Behav. Sci.*, 1968, *4*(3), 265-280.
A practical plan for educational revolution. In R. R. Goulet (Ed.), *Educational change: The reality and the promise*. (A report on the National Seminars on Innovation, Honolulu, July 1967.) New York: Citation Press, 1968, pp. 120-135.
Review of J. Kavanaugh's, *A modern priest looks at his outdated Church*. *Psychology Today*, 1968, p. 13.
To the Japanese reader. Introduction to a series of 18 volumes of Rogers' work translated into Japanese. Tokyo: Iwasaki Shoten Press, 1968.
With W. R. Coulson (Eds.), *Man and the science of man*. Columbus, Ohio: Charles E. Merrill Publishing Co., 1968.

1969

Being in relationship. In *Freedom to learn: A view of what education might become*. Columbus, Ohio: Charles E. Merrill Publishing Co., 1969.
Community: The group. *Psychology Today*, Del Mar, California: CRM Books, Inc., December 1969, 3.
Freedom to learn: A view of what education might became. Columbus, Ohio: Charles E. Merrill Publishing Co., 1969.
Graduate education in psychology: A passionate statement. In C. R. Rogers, *Freedom to learn: A view of what education might become*.
The increasing involvement of the psychologist in social problems: Some comments, positive and negative. *J. Appl. Behav. Sci.*, 1969, *5*, 3-7.
The intensive group experience. In *Psychology today: An introduction*. Del Mar, California: CRM Books Inc., 1969, pp. 539-555.
The person of tomorrow. Sonoma State College Pamphlet, 1969. Also in *Colorado Journal of Educational Research*, 1972, *12*(1), 30-32.
Self-directed change for educators: Experiments and implications. In E.

Morphet & D. L. Jesser (Eds.), *Preparing educators to meet emerging needs.* New York: Citation Press, Scholastic Magazine Inc., 1969.
Some personal learnings about interpersonal relationships. *Word*, November 1969, 7(2).

1970

Carl Rogers on encounter groups. New York: Harper & Row, 1970.
Foreword and Chapters 9,16,22,25,26,27. In J. T. Hart & T. M. Tomlinson (Eds.), *New direction in client-centered therapy.* Boston: Houghton Mifflin, 1970. (All have been published elsewhere, except the Foreword and Chapter 27, "Looking back and ahead: A conversation with Carl Rogers," conducted by J. T. Hart.)
Rogers can change. *Educate*, 1970, *3*(3), 19-23,33.
Views of USIU. *Association for Humanistic Psychology Newsletter*, October 1970, 7(1).

1971

Can schools grow persons? Editorial. *Educational Leadership*, 1971, *29*, 215-217.
Forget you are a teacher. Carl Rogers tells why. *Instructor* (Dansville, New York), 1971, *81*, 65-66.
Interview with Dr. Carl Rogers. In W. B. Frick (Ed.), *Humanistic Psychology: Interviews with Maslow, Murphy and Rogers*, Columbus, Ohio: Charles E. Merrill Co., 1971.
Psychological maladjustment vs. continuing growth. In *Developmental psychology.* Del Mar, California: CRM Books, Inc., 1971.
Some elements of effective interpersonal communication. *Washington State Journal of Nursing*, May/June 1971, pp. 3-11.
Facilitating encounter groups. *American Journal of Nursing*, 1971, *71*(2), 275-279.

1972

Becoming partners: Marriage and its alternatives. New York: Delacorte, 1972.
Bringing together ideas and feelings in learning. *Learning Today*, 1972, *5*, 32-43.
Comment on Brown and Tedeschi article. *J. Hum. Psychol.*, 1972, *12*(1), 16-21.
Introduction to *My experience in encounter group*, by H. Tsuge, Dean of Women at Japan Women's University, Tokyo, Japan. *Voices*, 1972, *8*(2), 69-77.
A research program in client-centered therapy. In S. R. Brown & D. J. Brenner (Eds.), *Science, psychology, and communication: Essays honoring William Stephenson.* New York: Teachers College Press, Teachers College, Columbia University, 1972, pp. 312-324.
Some social issues which concern me. *J. Hum. Psychol.*, 1972, *12*(2), 45-60.

Carl Rogers, gardener. *Human behavior*, November/December 1972, 1, 16 ff.
By J. T. Wood.
Foreword. In L. N. Solomon & B. Berzon (Eds.), *New perspectives on encoun-
ter groups*, San Francisco: Jossey-Bass, 1972.

1973

Comments on Pitts article. *J. Hum. Psychol.*, 1973, *13*, 83-84.
An encounter with Carl Rogers. In C. W. Kemper (Ed.), *Res Publica*, Clare-
mont Men's College, 1973, *1*(1), 41-51.
The good life as an ever-changing process. Ninth of newspaper series, *Ameri-
ca and the future of man*, published by the Regents of the University of
California, and distributed by Copley News Service.
The interpersonal relationship that helps schizophrenics. Contribution to
panel discussion, "Psychotherapy is effective with schizophrenics."
APA Convention, Montreal, August 28, 1973.
My philosophy of interpersonal relationships and how it grew. *J. Hum. Psy.*,
1973, *13*(2), 3-15.
Some new challenges. *American Psychologist*, 1973, *28*(5), 379-387.
To be fully alive. *Penney's Forum*, Spring/Summer 1973, 3.
With B. Meador. Client-centered therapy. In R. Corsini (ed.), Current Psy-
chotherapies. Itasca, Illinois: F. E. Peacock, 1973, pp. 119-165.
Entretien avec Carl Rogers. *Psychologie*, 1973, *6*, 57-65. By J. Mousseau.
Foreword. In the Japanese translation of *Carl Rogers on encounter groups*.
Tokyo, 1973.

1974

Can learning encompass both ideas and feelings? *Education*, 1974, *95*(2),
103-114.
Foreword. In H. Lyon's, *It's me and I'm here*. New York: Delacorte, 1974, pp.
xi-xiii.
Foreword. In A. dePeretti, *Pensee et Verite de Carl Rogers*. Toulouse: Privat,
1974, pp. 20-27.
Foreword. In Japanese translation of *Person to Person*. Tokyo, 1974.
In retrospect: Forty-six years. *American Psychologist*, 1974, *29*(2), 115-123.
Interview on "growth." In W. Oltmans (Ed.), *On growth: The crisis of exploring
population and resource depletion*. New York: G. P. Putman's Sons,
1974, pp. 197-205.
The project at Immaculate Heart: An experiment in self-directed change.
Education, 1974, *95*(2), 172-196.
Questions I would ask myself if I were a teacher. *Education*, 1974, *95*(2), 134-
139.
Remarks on the future of client-centered therapy. In D. A. Wexler & L. N.
Rice (Eds.), *Innovations in client-centered therapy*, New York: John
Wiley & Sons, 1974, pp. 7-13.
With J. K. Wood. The changing theory of client-centered therapy. In A.
Burton (Ed.), *Operational theories of personality*. New York:

Brunner/Mazel Inc., 1974, pp. 211-258.

1975

Client-centered psychotherapy. In A. M. Freedman, H. I. Kaplan, & B. J. Sadock (Eds.), *Comprehensive textbook of psychiatry*, Vol. II. Baltimore: Williams & Wilkins, 1975, pp. 1831-1843.
The emerging person: A new revolution. In R. I. Evans (Ed.), *Carl Rogers: The man and his ideas*. New York: Dutton, 1975, pp. 147-176.
Emphatic: An unappreciated way of being. *The Counseling Psychologist*, 1975, *5*(2), 2-10.
Foreword. In *To Thi Anh, Eastern & Western cultural values*. Manila, The Philippines: East Asian Pastoral Institute, 1975.
Interview. In R. I. Evans (Ed.), *Carl Rogers: The man and his ideas*. New York: Dutton, 1975.
An interview with Dr. Carl Rogers. *Practical Psychology for Physicians*, 1975, *2*(8), 16-24.

1976

Beyond the watershed of education. *Teaching-Learning Journal*, Winter/Spring 1976, pp. 43-49.
A dialogue on education and the control of human behavior. A six-cassette album of a dialogue held between Carl Rogers and B. F. Skinner in Duluth in 1962, edited by Gerald Gladstein, with a descriptive booklet, New York: Jeffrey, Norton, 1976.

1977

Beyond the watershed: And where now? *Educational Leadership*, 1977, *34*(8), 623-631.
Carl Rogers on Personal Power. New York: Delacorte, 1977.
Ellen West--And loneliness. In C. R. Rogers & R. L. Rosenberg, *A pessoa como centro*, Sao Paolo, Brazil: Editora Pedagogica e Universitaria Ltda., 1977.
Freedom to be: A person-centered approach. *Studies of the Person* (Japanese), 1977, *3*, 3-18. Japan Women's University, Department of Education.
Nancy mourns. In D. Nevill (Ed.), *Humanistic psychology: New frontiers*. New York: Gardner, 1977, pp. 111-116.
Personal power at work. *Psychology Today*, 1977, *10*(11), 60 ff.
The politics of education. *J. Hum. Educ.*, 1977, *1*(1):6-22.
Therapeut and Klient. Munich, West Germany: Kindler-Munchen, 1977. (Various papers translated from the English.)
Tribute to Professor Haruko Tsuge. *Studies of the Person* (Japanese), 1977, *3*, 35-38. Japan Women's University, Department of Education, Tokyo.
With T. L. Holdstock. Person-centered personality theory. In R. Corsini (Ed.), *Current personality theories*. Itasca, Illinois: F. R. Peacock, 1977,

pp. 125-151.
With R. L. Rosenberg. *A Pessoa Como Centro*. Sao Paolo, Brazil: Editora
    Pedagogica e Universitaria Ltda., 1977. (Introduction and chapters 2
    and 5 by Rosenberg. Other pages are translations of papers by Rog-
    ers.)
Carl Rogers: Giving people permission to be themselves. *Science*, 1977,
    198(4312), 32-33. By C. Holden.
Preface. In R. Fairfield, *Person-centered graduate education*. Elmhurst, Illi-
    nois: Hagle, 1977.

1978

Carl Rogers's Papers. In *The Quarterly Journal of the Library of Congress*,
    1978, *35*, 258-259. (This describes the collection of personal papers,
    tapes, films, etc., which, upon the invitation, Rogers donated to the
    Library of Congress.)
Do we need 'a' reality?" *Dawnpoint*, 1978, *1*(2), 6-9.
The formative tendency. *J. Hum. Psychol.*, 1978, *18*, 23-26.
From heart to heart: Some elements of effective personal communication.
    Marriage Encounter, 1978, *7*(2), 8-15.
The necessary and sufficient conditions of therapeutic personality change
    (1957). Abstract & commentary. *Current Contents*, 1978, *18*(27), 14.
    (No. 27 of "Citation Classics.")
With M. V. Bowen, J. Justyn, J. Kass, M. Miller, N. Rogers, & J. K. Wood.
    Evolving aspects of the person-centered workshop. *Self and Society*
    (England), 1978, *6*(2), 43-49.
Interview. *San Diego Union*, July 9, 1978.

1979

Foundations of the person-centered approach. *Education*, 1979, *100*(2), 98-
    107.
Groups in two cultures. *Personnel & Guidance Journal*, 1979, *38*(1), 11-15.
Some new directions: A personal view. In T. Hanna (Ed.), *Explorers of
    humankind*. San Francisco: Harper & Row, 1979, pp. 123-135.
With M. V. Bowen, M. Miller, & J. K. Wood. Learning in large groups: The
    implications for the future. *Education*, 1979, *100*(2), 108-116.
On becoming Carl Rogers. New York: Delacorte Press, 1979. By H. Kirschen-
    baum. (This biography includes many excerpts from Rogers' writings,
    from his adolescence days to age 76.)
Interview with Carl Rogers. In *Le Monde*, September 23, 1979.
My hopes for the workshop in Rome (Interview with A. Zucconi), *Pulsazione*,
    1979.

1980

A way of being. Boston: Houghton Mifflin, 1980.
Building person-centered communities: The implications for the future. In A.

Villoldo & K. Dychtwald (Eds.) *Revisioning human potential: Glimpses into the 21st century.*
Interview. *The Relator,* 1980, *23*(1).
Client-centered psychotherapy. In H. I. Kaplan, B. J. Sadock & A. M. Freedman (Eds.), *Comprehensive textbook of psychiatry,* Vol. III. Baltimore: Williams & Wilkins, 1980, pp. 2153-2168.
Growing old--or older and growing. *J. Hum. Psychol.,* 1980, *20*(4), 5-16.
Interview. *Los Angeles Times,* July 31, 1980.
Introduction. In the Japanese translation of *Carl Rogers on Personal Power,* 1980.
The person. *Association for Humanistic Psychology Newsletter,* May 1980, pp. 8-9.
Statement. A call to action: A report on AHP's 12-hour political party. *Association for Humanistic Psychology Newsletter* [special issue], February 1980.

1981

Introduction. In the Japanese translation of *Becoming partners: marriage and its alternatives,* 1981.
Introduction. In the German translation of a portion of *A way of being,* 1981.
Some unanswered questions. *Journey,* 1981, *1*(1), 1,4.
The foundation of the person-centered approach. *Dialectics and Humanism,* 1981, *1,* 5-16.
Notes on Rollo May. *Association for Humanistic Psychology Perspectives,* 1981, *2*(1).
Education: A personal activity. *Educational Change and Development* (Sheffield, England), 1981, *3*(3), 1-12.
Foreword--The formative tendency. In J. R. Royce & P. M. Leendert, *Humanistic psychology-Concepts and criticisms.* New York: Plenum, 1981, pp. vii-x.

1982

Freedom to learn for the 80's. *Association for Humanistic Psychology Perspective,* October 1982, pp. 20-21.
A psychologist looks at nuclear war: Its treat, its possible prevention. *J. Hum. Psychol.,* 1982, *22*(4), 9-21.
My politics. *Journey,* September 1982, *1*(6).
With J. Elliott-Kemp. *The effective teacher: A person-centered development guide.* Sheffield, England: PAVIC, 1982.
Zeitschrift fur personenzentrierta Psychologie und psychotherapy. Sonderdruck, Beltz, 75-77. ("My description of a person-centered approach").
Entrevista con Carl Rogers. *Anuario de Psicologia* (Departamento de Psicologia, Universidad de Barcelona), 1982, *27*(2), 111-115.
Reply to Rollo May's letter to Carl Rogers. *J. Hum. Psychol.,* 1982, *22*(4), 85-89.

1983

Freedom to learn for the 80's. Columbus, Ohio: Merrill, 1983.
A visit to Credo Mutwa. *Journey*, 1983, *2*(4), 1,4-5.
Um novo mundo-uma nova pessoa. In A. Fonseca (Ed.), *Em busca de vida.* Sao Paolo, Brazil: Summurs, 1983.
Carl Rogers speaks to Montessorians. *The NAMTA Quart.*, 1983, *8*(4), 11-15.
Dialogos con Carl Rogers. *Revista de Psiquiatria & Psicologia Humanista*, May 1983, (4).
I walk softly through life. *Voices*, 1983, *18*(4), 6-14.
I can't read. *Visualtek News*, Summer 1983.

1984

With R. Sanford. Client-centered psychotherapy. In H. I. Kaplan & B. J. Sadock (Eds.), *Comprehensive textbook of psychiatry*, Vol. IV, Baltimore: Williams & Wilkins, 1984, pp. 1374-1388.
Person-centered approach foundations. In R. Corsini (Ed.), *Encyclopedia of psychology*. New York: Wiley & Sons, 1984.
The new world person. *Odyssey* (S. Africa), 1984, *8*(2), 16-19.
With D. Ryback. One alternative to nuclear planetary suicide. (with D. Ryback), *The Counseling Psychologist*, 1984, *12*(2), 3-12.
Gloria-A historical note. In R. Levant & J. Shlien (Eds.), *Client-centered therapy and the person-centered approach*. New York: Praeger, 1984, pp. 403-425.
A way of meeting life (an interview). *The Laughing Man*, 1984, *5*(2), 22-23.
Interview. *Holistic Living News*, 1984-85, 7(3).

1985

La development de la personne. *Le Journal des Psychologies*, 1985, *23*, 10-12.
Toward a more human science of the person. *J. Hum. Psychol.*, 1985, *25*(4), 7-24.

1986

The rust workshop. *J. Hum. Psychol.*, 1986, *26*(3), 23-45.
What I learned from two research studies. In H. Kirschenbaum & V. L. Henderson (Eds.), *The Carl Rogers Reader*. Boston: Houghton Mifflin, 1989, pp. 203-211.
A client-centered/person-centered approach to therapy. In Kutash, I. & Wolf, A. (Eds.), *Psychotherapist's casebook*. San Francisco: Jossey-Bass, 1986, pp. 197-208.
Reflection of feelings and transference. *Person-Centered Review*, 1986, *1*, 375-377.

1987

Comments on the issue of equality in psychotherapy. *J. Hum. Psychol.*, 1987, 27(1), 38-40.
Inside the world of the Soviet professional. *Journal of Humanistic Psychology*, 1987, 27, 277-304.
On reaching 85. *Person-Centered Review*, 1987, 2, 150-152.

Works About Rogers

American Psychological Association. Award for distinguishing professional contributions: 1972. *American Psychologist* 28 (1973): 71-74.
Dallis, Constantine A. *The development of Rogerian thought and its implication for counselor education* (unpublished doctoral dissertation, University of Wisconsin-Madison, 1965).
Evans, Richard I. *Carl Rogers: The man and his ideas* (New York: Dutton, 1975).
Farson, Richard. Carl Rogers, quite revolutionary. *Education* 95 (1975): 197-203.
Frick, Willard B. *Humanistic psychology: Interviews with Maslow, Murphy and Rogers* (Columbus: Merrill, 1971).
Holden, Constance. Carl Rogers: Giving people permission to be themselves. *Science* 198,4312 (1977): 31-35.
Kirschenbaum, Howard. *On becoming Carl Rogers* (New York: Delacorte, 1979).
Kirschenbaum, Howard and Henderson, Valerie L. *The Carl Rogers reader* (Boston: Houghton Mifflin, 1989).
Kirschenbaum, Howard and Henderson, Valerie L. *Carl Rogers: Dialogues* (Boston: Houghton Mifflin, 1989).
dePeretti, Andre. *Pensee et verite de Carl Rogers* (Toulouse: Privat, 1974).
Wood, John T. Carl Rogers gardener. *Human Behavior*, Nov/Dec., 1972.

INDEX